PROP
(

MCSE Exam Notes™:
Internet Information Server 4

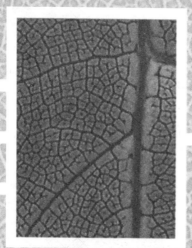

Matthew Strebe

San Francisco • Paris • Düsseldorf • Soest

Associate Publisher: Guy Hart-Davis
Contracts and Licensing Manager: Kristine Plachy
Acquisitions & Developmental Editor: Maureen Adams
Editor: Suzanne Goraj
Project Editor: Raquel Baker
Technical Editor: Matthew Fiedler
Book Designer: Bill Gibson
Electronic Publishing Specialist: Bill Gibson
Production Coordinator: Rebecca Rider
Indexer: Nancy Guenther
Cover Designer: Archer Design
Cover Photographer: FPG International

SYBEX is a registered trademark of SYBEX Inc.

Exam Notes is a trademark of SYBEX Inc.

TRADEMARKS: SYBEX has attempted throughout this book to distinguish proprietary trademarks from descriptive terms by following the capitalization style used by the manufacturer.

Microsoft, the Microsoft Internet Explorer logo, Windows, Windows NT, and the Windows logo are either registered trademarks or trademarks of Microsoft Corporation in the United States and/or other countries.

The author and publisher have made their best efforts to prepare this book, and the content is based upon final release software whenever possible. Portions of the manuscript may be based upon pre-release versions supplied by software manufacturer(s). The author and the publisher make no representation or warranties of any kind with regard to the completeness or accuracy of the contents herein and accept no liability of any kind including but not limited to performance, merchantability, fitness for any particular purpose, or any losses or damages of any kind caused or alleged to be caused directly or indirectly from this book.

SYBEX is an independent entity from Microsoft Corporation, and not affiliated with Microsoft Corporation in any manner. This publication may be used in assisting students to prepare for a Microsoft Certified Professional Exam. Neither Microsoft Corporation, its designated review company, nor SYBEX warrants that use of this publication will ensure passing the relevant exam. Microsoft is either a registered trademark or trademark of Microsoft Corporation in the United States and/or other countries.

Copyright ©1998 SYBEX Inc., 1151 Marina Village Parkway, Alameda, CA 94501. World rights reserved. No part of this publication may be stored in a retrieval system, transmitted, or reproduced in any way, including but not limited to photocopy, photograph, magnetic or other record, without the prior agreement and written permission of the publisher.

Library of Congress Card Number: 98-85869
ISBN: 0-7821-2303-1

Manufactured in the United States of America

10 9 8 7 6 5 4 3 2 1

Microsoft®
CERTIFIED PROFESSIONAL
Approved Study Guide

November 1, 1997

Dear SYBEX Customer:

Microsoft is pleased to inform you that SYBEX is a participant in the Microsoft®
Independent Courseware Vendor (ICV) program. Microsoft ICVs design, develop,
and market self-paced courseware, books, and other products that support Microsoft
software and the Microsoft Certified Professional (MCP) program.

To be accepted into the Microsoft ICV program, an ICV must meet set criteria. In
addition, Microsoft reviews and approves each ICV training product before
permission is granted to use the Microsoft Certified Professional Approved Study
Guide logo on that product. This logo assures the consumer that the product has
passed the following Microsoft standards:

- The course contains accurate product information.
- The course includes labs and activities during which the student can apply
  knowledge and skills learned from the course.
- The course teaches skills that help prepare the student to take corresponding
  MCP exams.

Microsoft ICVs continually develop and release new MCP Approved Study Guides.
To prepare for a particular Microsoft certification exam, a student may choose one or
more single, self-paced training courses or a series of training courses.

You will be pleased with the quality and effectiveness of the MCP Approved Study
Guides available from SYBEX.

Sincerely,

Holly Heath
ICV Account Manager
Microsoft Training & Certification

MICROSOFT INDEPENDENT COURSEWARE VENDOR PROGRAM

For Christy, Always.

Acknowledgments

This book would not exist without the tireless dedication of the people at Sybex: Neil Edde, Maureen Adams, Raquel Baker, Rebecca Rider, Bill Gibson, Matt Fiedler, and Suzanne Goraj. I'd also like to thank Charles Perkins, the co-author of *MCSE: Internet Information Server Study Guide 4*, from which so much of this book is drawn.

Table of Contents

Introduction

If you've purchased this book, you are probably chasing one of the Microsoft professional certifications: MCP, MCSE, or MCT. All of these are great goals, and they are also great career builders. Glance through any newspaper and you'll find employment opportunities for people with these certifications—these ads are there because finding qualified employees is a challenge in today's market. The certification means you know something about the product, but more importantly, it means you have the ability, determination, and focus to learn—the greatest skill any employee can have!

You've probably also heard all the rumors about how hard the Microsoft tests are—believe us, the rumors are true! Microsoft has designed a series of exams that truly test your knowledge of their products. Each test not only covers the materials presented in a particular class, it also covers the prerequisite knowledge for that course. This means two things for you—that first test can be a real hurdle and each test *should* get easier since you've studied the basics over and over.

This book has been developed in alliance with the Microsoft Corporation to give you the knowledge and skills you need to prepare for one of the key elective exams of the MCSE certification program: Exam 70-087. Reviewed and approved by Microsoft, this book provides a solid introduction to Microsoft networking technologies and will help you on your way to MCSE certification.

The Internet has caused more social change in a shorter time than any other technology in the history of modern innovation. Not even television approached the speed at which the Internet has been adopted into the business and personal lives of people around the world. Just as the telephone and then the fax became ubiquitous essentials for doing business, the e-mail address and Web site now differentiate the competitive from the soon-to-be-extinct.

Microsoft has determined that the Internet is fundamental to the success of all of their products. Windows NT now comes with Internet Information Server 4 (IIS4) for no additional charge. IIS4 is one of the premier Web servers, with a feature set as rich and powerful as any competitor's.

You will find very complete coverage of the Microsoft Internet Information Server 4.0 exam between these pages. This book has been condensed from *MCSE: Internet Information Server 4 Study Guide* for the professional who requires concentrated information about the exam itself rather than exhaustive coverage of IIS4. If you find yourself getting lost when you read this book, or requiring additional information to understand the technology, don't fret: *MCSE: Internet Information Server 4 Study Guide* is for you. It covers in depth what this volume takes for granted that you understand. If you find the IIS4 study guide a bit beyond you, start at the beginning of the MCSE series with *MCSE: Networking Essentials Study Guide* (or better yet, the boxed MCSE set and the boxed Internet Specialist set) and follow the exam track listed later in this introduction. You'll be an MCSE in no time!

Is This Book for You?

The MCSE Exam Notes books were designed to be succinct, portable exam review guides that can be used either in conjunction with a more complete study program (book, CBT courseware, classroom/ lab environment) or as an exam review for those who don't feel the need for more extensive test preparation. It isn't our goal to give the answers away, but rather to identify the topics on which you can expect to be tested and to provide sufficient coverage of these topics.

Perhaps you've been working with Microsoft networking technologies for years now. The thought of paying lots of money for a specialized MCSE exam preparation course probably doesn't sound too appealing. What can they teach you that you don't already know, right? Be careful, though. Many experienced network administrators have walked confidently into test centers only to walk sheepishly out of them after failing an MCSE exam. As they discovered, there's the Microsoft of the real world and the Microsoft of the MCSE exams. It's our goal with these Exam Notes books to show you where the two converge and where they diverge. After you've finished reading through this book, you should have a clear idea of how your understanding of the technologies involved matches up with the expectations of the MCSE testmakers in Redmond.

Or perhaps you're relatively new to the world of Microsoft networking, drawn to it by the promise of challenging work and higher salaries. You've just waded through an 800-page MCSE study guide or taken a class at a local training center. Lots of information to keep track of, isn't there? Well, by organizing the Exam Notes books according to the Microsoft exam objectives, and by breaking up the information into concise manageable pieces, we've created what we think is the handiest exam review guide available. Throw it in your briefcase and carry it to work with you. As you read through the book, you'll be able to identify quickly those areas you know best and those that require more in-depth review.

NOTE The goal of the Exam Notes series is to help MCSE candidates familiarize themselves with the subjects on which they can expect to be tested in the MCSE exams. For complete, in-depth coverage of the technologies and topics involved, we recommend the MCSE Study Guide series from Sybex.

This book (and series) is designed as a quick reference to the Microsoft exam for the professional administrator who is already experienced with Windows NT and Internet Information Server 4. It does not provide background detail on the technology beyond the scope of the exam. More complete treatments of Internet Information Server are contained in *MCSE: Internet Information Server 4 Study Guide*, which is designed for those familiar with Windows NT but not familiar with IIS or the Web.

How Is This Book Organized?

As mentioned above, this book is organized according to the official exam objectives list prepared by Microsoft for the Internet Information Server 4 (70-087) exam. The chapters coincide with the broad objectives groupings, such as Planning, Installation and Configuration, Monitoring and Optimization, and Troubleshooting. These groupings are also reflected in the organization of the MCSE exams themselves.

This book is based on Microsoft's official exam objectives—the objectives form the outline of this book. Within each chapter, the individual exam objectives are addressed in turn. And in turn, the objective sections are further divided according to the type of information presented.

NOTE In some chapters, some objective topics will be lightly covered in combination with others. In those cases, you'll be referred to another section or chapter for more thorough coverage of that topic.

Critical Information
This section presents the greatest level of detail on information that is relevant to the objective. This is the place to start if you're unfamiliar with or uncertain about the technical issues related to the objective.

Necessary Procedures
Here you'll find instructions for procedures that require a lab computer to complete. From installing operating systems to modifying configuration defaults, the information in these sections addresses the hands-on requirements for the MCSE exams. These are the tasks you'll be expected to perform in the exam's new console simulator.

NOTE Not every objective has procedures associated with it. For such objectives, the Necessary Procedures section has been left out.

Exam Essentials
In this section, we've put together a concise list of the most crucial topics that you'll need to comprehend fully prior to taking the MCSE exam. This section can help you identify the topics that might require more study on your part.

Key Terms and Concepts
Here we've compiled a mini-glossary of the most important terms and concepts related to the specific objective. You'll understand what all those technical words mean within the context of the related subject matter.

Sample Questions

For each objective, we've included a selection of questions similar to those you'll encounter on the actual MCSE exam. Answers and explanations are provided so you can gain some insight into the test-taking process and test your knowledge before you're in the hot seat.

NOTE For a more comprehensive collection of exam review questions, check out the MCSE Test Success series, also published by Sybex.

How Do You Become an MCSE?

Attaining Microsoft Certified Systems Engineer (MCSE) status is a challenge. The exams cover a wide range of topics and require dedicated study and expertise. This is, however, why the MCSE certificate is so valuable. If achieving the MCSE were too easy, the market would be quickly flooded by MCSEs and the certification would become meaningless. Microsoft, keenly aware of this fact, has taken steps to ensure that the certification means its holder is truly knowledgeable and skilled.

To become an MCSE, you must pass four core requirements and two electives. Most people select the following exam combination for the MCSE core requirements for the most current track:

Client Requirement

70-073: Implementing and Supporting Windows NT Workstation 4.0 or

70-064: Implementing and Supporting Microsoft Windows 95

Networking Requirement

70-058: Networking Essentials

Windows NT Server 4.0 Requirement

70-067: Implementing and Supporting Windows NT Server 4.0

Windows NT Server 4.0 in the Enterprise Requirement

70-068: Implementing and Supporting Windows NT Server 4.0 in the Enterprise

Electives

Some of the more popular electives include:

70-059: Internetworking Microsoft TCP/IP on Microsoft Windows NT 4.0

70-087: Implementing and Supporting Microsoft Internet Information Server 4.0

70-081: Implementing and Supporting Microsoft Exchange Server 5.5

70-026: System Administration for Microsoft SQL Server 6.5

70-027: Implementing a Database Design on Microsoft SQL Server 6.5

70-088: Implementing and Supporting Microsoft Proxy Server 2.0

70-079: Implementing and Supporting Microsoft Internet Explorer 4.0 by Using the Internet Explorer Administration Kit

---

TIP   This book is a part of a series of MCSE Exam Notes books, published by Network Press (SYBEX), that covers four core requirements and your choice of several electives—the entire MCSE track!

Where Do You Take the Exams?

You may take the exams at any one of more than 800 Sylvan Prometric Authorized Testing Centers around the world. For the location of a testing center near you, call (800) 755-EXAM (755-3926). Outside the United States and Canada, contact your local Sylvan Prometric Registration Center. You can also register for an exam with Sylvan Prometric via the Internet. The Sylvan site can be reached through the Microsoft Training and Certification site or at: http://www.slspro.com/msreg/microsoft.asp.

To register for a Microsoft Certified Professional exam:

1. Determine the number of the exam you want to take.

2. Register with Sylvan Prometric. At this point you will be asked for advance payment for the exam. At this writing, the exams are $100 each. Exams must be taken within one year of payment. You can schedule exams up to six weeks in advance or as late as one working day prior to the date of the exam. You can cancel or reschedule your exam if you contact Sylvan Prometric at least two working days prior to the exam. Same-day registration is available in some locations, although this is subject to space availability. Where same-day registration is available, you must register a minimum of two hours before test time.

3. After you receive a registration and payment confirmation letter from Sylvan Prometric, call a nearby Sylvan Prometric Testing Center to schedule your exam.

When you schedule the exam, you'll be provided with instructions regarding appointment and cancellation procedures, ID requirements, and information about the testing center location.

NOTE Beginning in June 1998, MCSE and MCPS candidates in the U.S. and Canada will be able to sign up to take the exams from Virtual University Enterprises (VUE) as well as Sylvan Prometric. To enroll at a VUE testing center, call toll-free in North America: (888) 837-8616; or visit VUE's web site at **www.vue.com/student-services**.

What Does the Internet Information Server 4 Exam Measure?

The IIS4 exam is primarily interested in your ability to install and configure IIS4 to serve Web and FTP sites, and, to a lesser degree, manage SMTP, NNTP, and Index Server. There is a section of the exam which measures your ability to configure IIS in a simulated MMC—you must have actual experience on a Windows NT Server running IIS to pass this exam.

How Does Microsoft Develop the Exam Questions?

Microsoft's exam development process consists of eight mandatory phases. The process takes an average of seven months and contains more than 150 specific steps. The phases of Microsoft Certified Professional exam development are listed here.

Phase 1: Job Analysis

Phase 1 is an analysis of all the tasks that make up the specific job function based on tasks performed by people who are currently performing the job function. This phase also identifies the knowledge, skills, and abilities that relate specifically to the certification for that performance area.

Phase 2: Objective Domain Definition

The results of the job analysis provide the framework used to develop exam objectives. The development of objectives involves translating the job function tasks into a comprehensive set of more specific and measurable knowledge, skills, and abilities. The resulting list of objectives, or the objective domain, is the basis for the development of both the certification exams and the training materials.

NOTE The outline of all Exam Notes books is based upon the official exam objectives lists published by Microsoft. Objectives are subject to change without notification. We advise that you check the Microsoft Training & Certification Web site (www.microsoft.com\ train_cert\) for the most current objectives list.

Phase 3: Blueprint Survey

The final objective domain is transformed into a blueprint survey in which contributors—technology professionals who are performing the applicable job function—are asked to rate each objective. Based on the contributors' input, the objectives are prioritized and weighted. The actual exam items are written according to the prioritized objectives. The blueprint survey phase helps determine which objectives to measure, as well as the appropriate number and types of items to include on the exam.

Phase 4: Item Development

A pool of items is developed to measure the blueprinted objective domain. The number and types of items to be written are based on the results of the blueprint survey. During this phase, items are reviewed and revised to ensure that they are:

- Technically accurate

- Clear, unambiguous, and plausible

- Not biased toward any population, subgroup, or culture

- Not misleading or tricky

- Testing at the correct level of Bloom's Taxonomy

- Testing for useful knowledge, not obscure or trivial facts

Items that meet these criteria are included in the initial item pool.

Phase 5: Alpha Review and Item Revision

During this phase, a panel of technical and job function experts reviews each item for technical accuracy, then answers each item, reaching consensus on all technical issues. Once the items have been verified as technically accurate, they are edited to ensure that they are expressed in the clearest language possible.

Phase 6: Beta Exam

The reviewed and edited items are collected into a beta exam pool. During the beta exam, each participant has the opportunity to respond to all of the items in the pool. Based on the responses of all beta participants, Microsoft performs a statistical analysis to verify the validity of the exam items and to determine which items will be used in the certification exam. Once the analysis has been completed, the items are distributed into multiple parallel forms, or versions, of the final certification exam.

Phase 7: Item Selection and Cut-Score Setting

The results of the beta exam are analyzed to determine which items should be included in the certification exam based on many factors, including item difficulty and relevance. Generally, the desired items are answered correctly by 25 percent to 90 percent of the beta exam candidates. This helps ensure that the exam consists of a variety of difficulty levels, from somewhat easy to extremely difficult.

Also during this phase, a panel of job function experts determines the cut score (minimum passing score) for the exam. The cut score differs from exam to exam because it is based on an item-by-item determination of the percentage of candidates who would be expected to answer the item correctly. The experts determine the cut score in a group session to increase the reliability.

Phase 8: Live Exam

Once all the other phases are complete, the exam is ready. Microsoft Certified Professional exams are administered by Sylvan Prometric.

Tips for Taking Your IIS4 Exam

Here are some general tips for taking your exam successfully:

- Practice the necessary procedures in this book the day before taking your exam.

- Get a good night's sleep prior to the exam.

- Eat breakfast. Drink a single caffeinated beverage if your diet and medical condition allow.

- Arrive early at the exam center so you can relax and review your study materials, particularly tables and lists of exam-related information. You can study this book while you wait, but you won't be allowed to take it with you to the test console.

- Read the questions carefully. Don't be tempted to jump to an early conclusion. Make sure you know *exactly* what the question is asking before selecting an answer.

- Don't leave any unanswered questions. They count against you.

- When answering multiple-choice questions you're not sure about, use a process of elimination to get rid of the obviously incorrect questions first. This will improve your odds if you need to make an educated guess.

- Because the hard questions will eat up the most time, save them for last. You can move forward and backward through the exam.

- This test has many exhibits (pictures). It can be difficult, if not impossible, to view both the questions and the exhibit simulation on the 14- and 15-inch screens usually found at the testing centers. Call around to each center and see if they have 17-inch monitors available. If they don't, perhaps you can arrange to bring in your own. Failing this, some have found it useful to quickly draw the diagram on the scratch paper provided by the testing center and use the monitor to view just the question.

- Many participants run out of time before they are able to complete the test. If you are unsure of the answer to a question, you may want to choose one of the answers, mark the question, and go on—an unanswered question does not help you. Once your time is up, you cannot go on to another question. However, you can remain on the question you are on indefinitely when the time runs out. Therefore, when you are almost out of time, go to a question you think you can figure out—given enough time—and work until you feel you have got it (or the night security guard boots you out!).

- You are allowed to use the Windows calculator during your test. However, it may be better to memorize a table of the subnet addresses and to write it down on the scratch paper supplied by the testing center before you start the test.

Once you have completed an exam, you will be given immediate, online notification of your pass or fail status. You will also receive a printed Examination Score Report indicating your pass or fail status and your exam results by section. (The test administrator will give you the printed score report.) Test scores are automatically forwarded to Microsoft within five working days after you take the test. You do not need to send your score to Microsoft. If you pass the exam, you will receive confirmation from Microsoft, typically within two to four weeks.

Contact Information

To find out more about Microsoft Education and Certification materials and programs, to register with Sylvan Prometric, or to get other useful information, check the following resources. Outside the United States or Canada, contact your local Microsoft office or Sylvan Prometric testing center.

Microsoft Certified Professional Program—(800) 636-7544

Call the MCPP number for information about the Microsoft Certified Professional program and exams, and to order the latest Microsoft Roadmap to Education and Certification.

Sylvan Prometric testing centers—(800) 755-EXAM

Contact Sylvan to register to take a Microsoft Certified Professional exam at any of more than 800 Sylvan Prometric testing centers around the world.

Microsoft Certification Development Team—Web: http://www .microsoft.com/Train_Cert/mcp/examinfo/certsd.htm

Contact the Microsoft Certification Development Team through their Web site to volunteer for participation in one or more exam development phases or to report a problem with an exam. Address written correspondence to: Certification Development Team, Microsoft Education and Certification, One Microsoft Way, Redmond, WA 98052.

**Microsoft TechNet Technical Information Network—
(800) 344-2121**
This is an excellent resource for support professionals and system administrators. Outside the United States and Canada, call your local Microsoft subsidiary for information.

How to Contact the Authors

You may contact the author of this book through the publisher:

SYBEX Inc.
Customer Service Department
1151 Marina Village Parkway
Alameda, CA 94501
(510) 523-8233
Fax: (510) 523-2373
e-mail: info@sybex.com

Or you may send e-mail to: `mstrebe@aol.com`.

How to Contact the Publisher

Sybex welcomes reader feedback on all of their titles. Visit the Sybex Web site at `www.sybex.com` for book updates and additional certification information. You'll also find online forms to submit comments or suggestions regarding this or any other Sybex book.

CHAPTER

1

Planning

Microsoft Exam Objectives Covered in This Chapter:

▶ **Choose a security strategy for various situations. Security considerations include:** *(pages 3 – 15)*
- Controlling anonymous access
- Controlling access to known users and groups
- Controlling access by host or network
- Configuring SSL to provide encryption and authentication schemes
- Identifying the appropriate balance between security requirements and performance requirements

▶ **Choose an implementation strategy for an Internet site or an intranet site for stand-alone servers, single-domain environments, and multiple-domain environments. Tasks include:** *(pages 15 – 23)*
- Resolving host header name issues by using a HOSTS file or DNS, or both
- Choosing the appropriate operating system on which to install IIS

▶ **Choose the appropriate technology to resolve specified problems. Technology options include:** *(pages 23 – 30)*
- WWW service
- FTP service
- Microsoft Transaction Server
- Microsoft SMTP Service
- Microsoft NNTP Service
- Microsoft Index Server
- Microsoft Certificate Server

Planning covers those decisions you should make before you install and implement a Web site based on Internet Information Server. This includes how you will properly secure your Web site, how you will integrate the server with either the Internet or the rest of your network, and which services you need to install to achieve your goals. Planning is the first step in any integration endeavor. For IIS, you must determine which services you will provide and what your security requirements are.

SEE ALSO You may also want to study Chapter 2, "Planning Your Site," in *MCSE: Internet Information Server 4 Study Guide* by Matthew Strebe and Charles Perkins (Sybex, 1998).

Choose a security strategy for various situations. Security considerations include:

- Controlling anonymous access
- Controlling access to known users and groups
- Controlling access by host or network
- Configuring SSL to provide encryption and authentication schemes
- Identifying the appropriate balance between security requirements and performance requirements

Security is critical to Internet service, and often overlooked or incorrectly implemented. Hackers break into Web sites regularly, and penetrate even further into corporate networks either through the Web site or by using information gleaned therefrom. With all this bad press, one might wonder if it's possible to work safely on the Web. It is—if you plan for security from the very beginning.

This objective covers the major security features of both IIS4 and Windows NT itself. IIS4 is an application that runs on and relies upon the security foundation provided by Windows NT. If you don't secure Windows NT, IIS4 will not be secure.

SEE ALSO *NT Network Security* by Matthew Strebe, Charles Perkins, and Michael Moncur (Sybex, 1998) is an excellent volume that covers all aspects of security, including firewalls and other protective measures, specific tactics used by hackers, and numerous ways that Internet sites can be compromised.

Critical Information

Access to your Web site and its various areas can be controlled using IIS service security and using NT file system security. IIS service security is implemented by the IIS application, whereas NTFS security is controlled by the operating system.

WARNING NTFS security is not available on volumes formatted with the FAT file system. For this reason, you should only use the NT file system for storing Internet sites.

You will also need to determine which parts of your site, if any, need to be encrypted when flowing over the public Internet. Connection encryption is performed using the Secure Socket Layer (SSL).

IIS Service Security

When you control access using IIS service security, you are relying upon the IIS service to limit access based on directory location, not user identity. With IIS service security, you can choose to permit:

- Read access per directory
- Write access per directory
- Script execution per directory
- Application execution per directory
- Directory browsing per Web site

- Indexing by Index Server per Web site

These permissions are controlled by IIS. For each access to your site, IIS checks the service permissions for the specified directory in the meta-base (a high-speed registry-like construct which will be explained later) and either grants the access or returns an error message, depending upon the service security settings. Figure 1.1 shows the IIS service security settings dialog box.

FIGURE 1.1: IIS service security settings

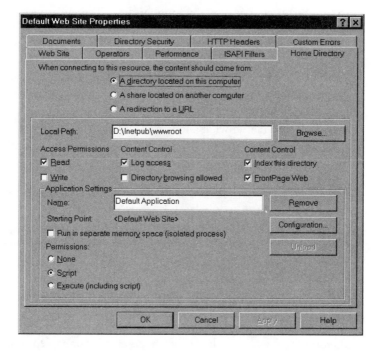

SEE ALSO Chapters 7 and 9 of *MCSE: Internet Information Server 4 Study Guide* contain more detailed information on IIS service security.

NT File System Security

When you control access using NTFS security, you are relying upon the operating system (Windows NT) to limit access based on the account credentials of the user requesting access. Every resource (file or directory in this case) on an NTFS-formatted volume has an access control list (ACL) containing a number of access control entries (ACEs) which consist of a specific permission and an account that receives that permission. An ACE in the ACL of a resource must specify both the requested access and either the account or a group of which the account is a member in order for a user to be granted access to that resource. Because any number of ACEs may appear in an ACL, and because accounts are normally members of more than one group, conflicting permissions may occur.

Permitted access is always cumulative. If read access is allowed by one group membership, and write access is allowed by another, the account will have read and write access. The special No Access permission will deny access no matter what allowed permissions exist. This permission is used to revoke any cumulative access that occurs due to multiple group memberships.

For example, if user account JANET wishes to gain read access to a file called DEFAULT.HTM, the ACL attached to DEFAULT.HTM must contain an ACE that specifies the JANET:READ permission, or GROUP:READ if JANET is a member of GROUP. However, if an ACE specifying NEWUSERS:NO_ACCESS is encountered and JANET is a member of NEWUSERS, then the account will be denied access no matter what other permissions are encountered.

NTFS permissions are inherited from the permissions assigned to the directory that contains the file when it is created or copied. When files are moved, the ACL does not change, because a move only consists of an update to the file's location in the directory tables; thus the file's permissions may not be the same as those of the containing directory. True moves only occur from one location within a volume to another. When a file is moved between volumes, the file is actually copied to the new location and then deleted from the original location. In this case, the ACL is changed according to the rules for a copy.

You can use NT file system security to control security for your Web site because Web site users are logged onto the server using a standard user account. If the user account has no access to the site files, IIS will return an error message rather than returning the Web site. Figure 1.2 shows NTFS security properly configured to secure a Web site.

F I G U R E 1.2: NT file system security settings

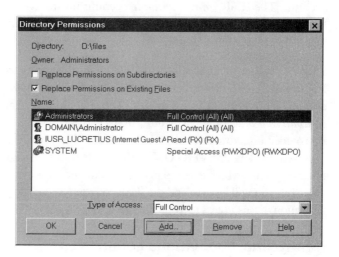

TIP   NTFS permissions are the most secure (and easiest) way to secure your Web site. Use NTFS permissions as your primary security method.

SEE ALSO   Chapter 5 of *MCSE: Internet Information Server 4 Study Guide* contains more detailed information on NTFS and account-based security.

Controlling Anonymous Access

Controlling anonymous access is performed by limiting the NTFS security permissions of the IUSR_*computername* account. The IUSR_*computername* account (*computername* is replaced with the name of your computer) is created during the installation of Internet Information Server. When an Internet user attaches to your site using anonymous credentials, IIS logs that user in using the IUSR_*computername* account. The IUSR_*computername* account must have the right to log on locally to the Web server, a right that is granted automatically when IIS creates the account.

IIS does not change the access control lists of any files or directories when it is installed. This means that by default, the IUSR_*computername* account is not granted access to your Web site. However, the IUSR_*computername* account is a member of the EVERYONE group, so access is provided under those credentials by default. However, if you have removed the default EVERYONE:FULL CONTROL ACE from your NT file system (which is mandatory if you intend to provide any real security), you will have to add the IUSR_*computername* account to provide anonymous access to your site files.

Controlling Anonymous Logon

In addition to the IUSR_*computername* account security, IIS can be configured using IIS service security to grant or deny access to a Web site based on anonymous credentials. For each directory or virtual directory, IIS allows you to choose whether you will accept anonymous credentials, require Basic Authentication, or require Windows NT Challenge/Response authentication. These permissions are generally established per site using the following guidelines:

- **Allow Anonymous Access** is used for public Internet sites and informational intranet/extranet sites. Anonymous access does not transmit a password across the network.

- **Basic Authentication** is used for membership Internet sites and intranet/extranet sites in a cross-platform network. Basic authentication transmits a clear text (unencrypted) password across the network.

- **Windows NT Challenge/Response** is used for intranets/extranets where all clients run Microsoft operating systems and where security is of paramount importance. Windows NT Challenge/Response transmits a hashed password across the network.

Internet Explorer will automatically attempt to log you on using the highest available security. This means that passwords may be transmitted across your network without your knowledge. For this reason, you should only enable those authentication techniques you intend to allow, and for anonymous sites you should not enable higher security. Figure 1.3 shows the IIS service security settings used to control authentication settings for a Web site.

F I G U R E 1.3: Controlling authentication

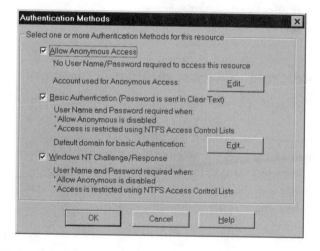

Controlling Access to Known Users and Groups

Controlling access to various accounts is performed using NTFS security, not IIS service-based security. If you want to control access to a Web site based on user account, simply assign NTFS permissions for the files and directories that make up that Web site. Remember that anonymous access is controlled using the IUSR_*computername* account.

When a client's Web browser is presented with content that it cannot access due to NTFS security, it will automatically prompt the user for a logon name and password using the most secure method supported by both the browser and the server. If you have configured security on the site not to accept Basic Authentication, only those users using Internet Explorer will be able to authenticate using NT Challenge/Response. If you've configured the directory to accept only anonymous connections, or if the user fails to log on correctly, IIS will return an access denied error message.

TIP To require a logon for a Web page, remove the IUSR_ *computername* account and any groups it is a member of (like EVERYONE) from the permissions list for the HTML files that make up the site or from the directory they're contained in. Make sure that IIS service security allows either Basic Authentication or NT Challenge/Response authentication, or both.

Controlling Access by Host or Network

Controlling access by host or network is accomplished through IIS service-based security. IIS can determine the IP address of each connected client, and can use the IP address to determine on a host-by-host or network-by-network (IP domain) basis whether or not to complete a transaction with a client. You can restrict or grant access based on either the IP address of a host or the network IP address with subnet mask of an IP domain.

You will use IP-based restrictions to supplement other security procedures. You can block access to any IP host or network of hosts based on either the IP address, a block of IP addresses specified by a net mask, or by the domain name of the host or network. Figure 1.4 shows the dialog box used to grant or deny access to computers based on their IP address.

FIGURE 1.4: IP security restrictions

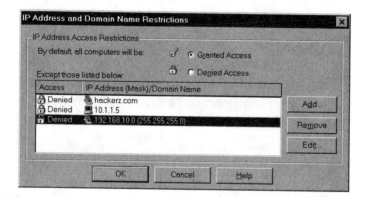

WARNING Using the domain name to block access to your site forces your Web server to perform a DNS lookup for every access to the site. This kills performance and is unnecessary since you can simply resolve the domain name to an IP address or domain manually by using the `nslookup` command at the MS-DOS prompt.

Configuring SSL to Provide Encryption and Authentication Schemes

Secure Socket Layer is an alternative TCP/IP-based connection method that encrypts the communication channel between the host and the client to ensure privacy. SSL is used to encrypt those areas of your Web site that transmit or receive privileged or sensitive information. Because encryption requires considerable compute resources, using SSL will reduce the overall performance of your Web server. You use Certificate Server to generate encryption keys for SSL.

There's no reason to encrypt all communications using SSL. You should only encrypt those portions of your Web site where sensitive or privileged information such as credit card numbers or passwords is transmitted. Since SSL requires considerable processing when it is in use, it reduces the number of users your Web server will be able to handle.

SEE ALSO Chapter 9 of *MCSE: Internet Information Server 4 Study Guide* contains more detailed information on SSL and Certificate Server.

Identifying the Appropriate Balance between Security Requirements and Performance Requirements

Security is always a trade-off. Security is naturally opposed to performance and ease of use because a more secure system is usually harder to use and always requires more compute power than a less secure or non-secure system. Your security requirements will vary greatly depending upon what you want to use your site for.

Most IIS installations will serve in one of three major environments:

- **Internet** security is the most difficult to correctly implement because account-based security is generally not used, in order to allow public access. Internet sites are also the target of far more hacking activity than intranet sites. Security must be implemented on an IIS service basis through mechanisms like directory access permissions and IP address restriction.

- **Extranet** security (which includes membership Internet sites) is harder to implement than that for intranets but easier than that for Internet sites. Because the identity of each user is known, you can use NTFS access permissions to lock down your site as necessary. However, the cross-platform requirement forces the use of Basic Authentication, which is less secure than NT Challenge/Response.

- **Intranet** security is the most secure, the easiest to implement, and the least likely to require elaborate methods. Since users are already logged into your network, they are already participating in domain security. You can use NTFS access permissions and secure authentication to lock down your intranet site.

Your security requirements will vary depending upon your exact situation. Understanding all the security options available will help you determine what your security requirements are. Understanding the performance impact of the security settings you implement will help you achieve a balance of acceptable performance and acceptable security.

Exam Essentials

Security is a major topic on the exam. Know exactly how account-based security works, and understand how to set up IP-based address restriction and IIS service security.

Know the difference between NTFS security and IIS service-based security. NTFS secures on a user account basis. IIS secures on access type, host, and network bases.

Know when to use NTFS-based security. Use NTFS-based security whenever your security requirements will change depending upon who is logged on.

Know when to use IIS service-based security. Use IIS service-based security for security that doesn't change no matter who's logged on.

Know how to control authentication. You can determine on a per-site basis what type of authentication will be used to gain access: anonymous, Basic Authentication, or Windows NT Challenge/Response.

Know when to use SSL to encrypt communications. Use Secure Socket Layer to encrypt the transmission of sensitive data across the Internet.

Key Terms and Concepts

Authentication: A method used to verify the identity of a user. Various authentication methods exist, with various levels of secure information exchange and software compatibility.

New Technology File System (NTFS) Security: Protects objects like files and directories on an account-by-account basis, allowing users with sufficient permissions access while denying access to those without.

Secure Socket Layer (SSL): Provides secure IP-based communications using high-speed encryption. Unlike other encryption schemes, SSL works with any service that uses TCP/IP.

Sites: Collections of HTML files, scripts, and applications with a consistent feel that together compose a coherent Internet property. A single server can host any number of sites.

Sample Questions

1. A client is worried about the possibility that credit card numbers could be intercepted while being routed through the Internet. Which security service is appropriate to secure against this sort of loss?

   A. NTFS security

   B. IIS service-based security

   C. Secure Socket Layer

   D. IP-based access restriction

   Answer: C. Secure Socket Layer encrypts information during transmission.

2. A client is worried about the possibility that hackers may gain access to their Internet server and compromise a list of credit card accounts stored there. Which security service should you rely upon to secure against this sort of loss?

   A. NTFS security

   B. IIS service-based security

   C. Secure Socket Layer

   D. IP-based access restriction

Answer: A. NTFS security is the most secure way to protect information on an Internet server. IIS service-based security will also work, but is less reliable and cannot discriminate based on user account.

3. You've noticed that a group of hackers routinely attempt to hack into your Web server. They all source from the same Class B network. What security service can you use to block access from this network?

   A. NTFS security

   B. IIS service-based security

   C. Secure Socket Layer

   D. IP-based access restriction

   Answer: D. IP-based access restriction allows you to grant or deny access to users based on IP address or network.

Choose an implementation strategy for an Internet site or an intranet site for stand-alone servers, single-domain environments, and multiple-domain environments. Tasks include:

- Resolving host header name issues by using a HOSTS file or DNS, or both
- Choosing the appropriate operating system on which to install IIS

This objective is worded strangely, and might lead one to believe that Microsoft thinks you should understand NT security domain concepts as they apply to the Internet. In fact, NT security domains have very little to do with implementing Internet sites beyond their effect on NT file system security. This objective actually concerns Internet domains, interdomain communication, and name resolution.

Name resolution is perhaps the biggest difference between single- and multiple-domain TCP/IP networks. It doesn't have to be a head-ache—if you install the right services for your enterprise, name resolution is easy and pretty much hassle-free.

Critical Information

Preparing to host Internet sites means preparing a well structured TCP/IP network. And whether or not you have a large network, you'll probably be attaching your servers to the Internet, which in itself is a large network, so you will have to be familiar with name resolution (which you normally don't need to worry about on smaller networks).

The two name services provided in Windows NT 4 are the Domain Name Service (DNS) used on the Internet and the Windows Internet Naming Service (WINS) used in Windows TCP/IP networks.

SEE ALSO Chapter 4 of *MCSE: Internet Information Server 4 Study Guide* contains more detailed information on DNS and WINS.

Choosing the Appropriate Operating System

Versions of IIS exist for both Windows NT Server and Windows NT Workstation. When installed on Windows NT Workstation, IIS is called Peer Web Services. A similar product for Windows 95 exists called Personal Web Server. Peer Web Services is limited to 10 connections, so it is worthless for all but the smallest intranets. Windows 95 is not a stable operating system and should not be considered for any serious Web site. For any business application, you should only consider installing IIS on Windows NT Server.

Domain Name Service

IP addresses are difficult for humans to remember, and for that reason the Domain Name System (DNS) was established. DNS allows you to use a human-readable name in place of an IP address nearly anywhere an IP address is accepted for input. When the name is provided, DNS will resolve the IP address, and a TCP/IP link can then be established with the target host.

DNS is a distributed database of IP address names maintained for the Internet by InterNIC, a not-for-profit organization dedicated to this task and currently operated by Network Solutions, Inc. For a domain name to be resolved on the Internet, it must be registered with InterNIC. For instance, microsoft.com is registered with InterNIC to point to Microsoft's DNS servers. Non-U.S. domain name registration is handled by a local naming authority similar to InterNIC.

Hosts within a domain can be added by the organization without further InterNIC registration. For instance, the four servers named www.microsoft.com, www1.microsoft.com, ftp.microsoft.com, and support.microsoft.com need only be registered by the DNS server maintained by Microsoft. The basic process for resolving a DNS name is as follows:

1. Host requests DNS name resolution from its DNS server (statically assigned through the Networking control panel or assigned by Dynamic Host Configuration Protocol [DHCP]) by providing the fully qualified domain name (for example, support.microsoft.com).

2. DNS server checks its database. Assuming no matching entry for support.microsoft.com, it then attempts to resolve microsoft.com. Assuming no matching entry, it resolves com to the InterNIC root DNS server.

3. DNS server sends domain name (support.microsoft.com) to root DNS server. Root server knows only microsoft.com (the only name registered), which it sends back to requesting DNS server.

4. DNS server queries DNS server microsoft.com with support
.microsoft.com. DNS server microsoft.com responds with specific IP address.

5. DNS server replies to host with IP address for support.microsoft
.com and adds entry to its locally cached database. Future name resolution for this address will be provided immediately.

6. Host establishes TCP/IP connection with IP address for support
.microsoft.com

Windows Internet Naming Service

WINS is a service similar to DNS that is designed to work with Microsoft's NetBIOS name browser service for Windows networks that span multiple IP domains. Prior to the use of TCP/IP in Windows networks, computer names were simply broadcast on the network. All computers in the network cached names as they were broadcast, so that after a few minutes each host would have a complete list of names for computers on its network. With protocols like NetBEUI and NWLink/IPX, this system works fine, since all hosts on a network will receive all broadcasts.

With TCP/IP, hosts on different subnetworks do not receive broadcasts because routers do not forward TCP/IP broadcasts. For this reason, computers have no way to resolve names for computers on other networks. WINS solves this problem by maintaining a master list of Windows computer names on a WINS server. Each host knows the IP address of the WINS server and can simply request name resolution if a name is unknown. Unlike DNS, WINS does not rely upon name registration—rather, browser computers automatically discover Windows names when they are broadcast on their respective networks and forward those names to the WINS server for inclusion in the WINS database. For this reason, WINS requires no maintenance once it's properly set up and as long as the database is not accidentally corrupted.

HOSTS Files

HOSTS files are simply text files stored on each client that list computer names and domain names along with their respective IP addresses. A computer can check its HOSTS file to resolve names if a name service is unavailable or unable to do so. HOSTS files are checked before a DNS or WINS resolve is attempted, so you can actually override DNS or WINS registered names if you need to for testing purposes.

HOSTS files are difficult to keep up to date because every HOSTS file on every client must be changed each time a new name is added or updated. For this reason, HOSTS files are largely obsolete. HOSTS files remain useful for debugging name resolution issues and for situations where only a small number of computers will ever be addressed.

TIP   Use HOSTS files to check your IIS server's host headers before you actually "go live" on the Internet. From the client you're using to check your Web site, simply list all the domain names your server will respond to and see if your various sites respond the way they should.

Necessary Procedures

The procedures for this objective are really about troubleshooting— and they'll be covered in more detail in the troubleshooting chapter at the end of this book. Installation issues only occur when you set up your server for the first time. This section discusses ways you can test the host header functionality of your IIS server before you go live on the Internet. There's also a procedure for choosing the correct operating system, but that's pretty much a no-brainer: Windows NT Server 4.

Resolving Host Header Name Issues by Using a HOSTS File or DNS, or Both

Once you've created your Web site and you want to test it to make sure everything's functioning correctly, it's likely you'll need to see whether or not the host headers feature of IIS is working correctly. There are two ways you can do this:

1. Install the DNS service and add entries for each host name you'll serve. This works only if the domain names will be postfixed with your company's domain name when the server is live on the Internet (e.g.: *yourclient.yourcompany*.com).

2. On the client you want to test from, create a HOSTS file and add entries for each host name you'll serve. This works well in any circumstance, and is easy both to set up and to remove.

The following procedure will show you how to use the HOSTS file to check host header functionality before your server goes live on the Internet:

1. Using a text editor, open the file `c:\winnt\system32\drivers\ etc\hosts` on the client you'll be using to browse from.

2. Add an entry to the bottom of the file by typing the current IP address of your server, a tab character, and the domain name you wish to test.

3. Repeat step 2 for each domain name you want to serve.

4. Open your Web browser and enter one of the host names you've set up in step 2. Your computer should resolve to the IP address of your Internet server and open the Web page that matches the site you've set up for host headers.

Choosing the Appropriate Operating System on Which to Install IIS

Install IIS4 on Windows NT Server 4. NT Workstation can support only 10 simultaneous connections, and no other Microsoft operating system is stable enough to function as a Web server.

Exam Essentials

The only information about this objective that you need to know concerns name resolution.

Understand name resolution. Know the different ways Windows names and Internet domain names are resolved in both single-domain and multiple-domain environments.

Understand the purpose and function of Domain Name Service. Understand what happens when domain names are used to refer to computers, how the domain name process resolves to an IP address, and how and when to implement DNS in your network.

Understand how WINS works and how it differs from DNS. Understand the WINS browsing process, how to implement WINS in your environment, and how WINS and DNS differ.

Key Terms and Concepts

Domain Name Service (DNS): The TCP/IP service that is used to query the InterNIC's (or a private network's) distributed database of Internet domain names.

HOSTS file: A text file that is stored on a client computer and lists domain names and their associated IP addresses for situations where DNS or WINS are either not available or not efficient.

Name resolution: The process of looking up a domain name to retrieve the associated IP address, much the way one looks up a person's name to obtain their telephone number.

Windows Internet Name Service (WINS): The NetBIOS service that is used to query a Windows NT domain's database of Windows computer names.

Sample Questions

1. You've added a second Ethernet subnetwork to your network. Both Ethernet segments are attached directly to a single server through separate network adapters. Clients on both networks can access the server properly, and they can access shares from clients on the Ethernet subnetwork, but you can't get client shares

working between subnetworks even though you've got routing enabled and properly configured. What's the easiest way to solve this problem?

A. Create a HOSTS file listing all computers on your network and their IP addresses. Copy this file to each client computer.

B. Install the DNS service on your server and establish a database of all computer names and their associated IP addresses.

C. Register your client names with InterNIC.

D. Install WINS on your server.

Answer: D. Installing WINS will solve this problem with the least amount of effort, although A and B will also work.

2. You want to set up the following servers to respond on the Internet: `digiwidge.com` for mail service, `www.digiwidge.com` for Web service, and `ftp.digiwidge.com` for file transfers. Which answer describes the necessary steps?

A. Install DNS on `digiwidge.com`, create entries for the other servers.

B. Install WINS on `digiwidge.com`.

C. Install DNS on `digiwidge.com`, register IP address for `digiwidge.com` with InterNIC, create entries for the other server.

D. E-mail the IP address for `digiwidge.com` to all Internet users for inclusion in their HOSTS files.

Answer: C. You must register at least your DNS server's IP address with InterNIC, and then you can create entries for your remaining servers on it.

3. You've set up a new Internet server with Windows NT, IIS, and the site files for 15 of your customers. You want to use host headers (a method for assigning domain names to Web sites on a single server) to distinguish between the sites since your server has only one IP address. What is the easiest method to test host headers functionality while you are using a temporary IP address without affecting other users on your network or the Internet?

A. Update your company's DNS server with new entries for the temporary Internet server.

B. Create a HOSTS file with the domain names and temporary IP address on the machine you'll browse from.

C. Manually add entries to the WINS database on your WINS server.

D. Use InterNIC's temporary IP address assignment facility to create "short period" IP addresses.

Answer: B. HOSTS files are great for temporary assignments and testing, especially since they affect only the client that has been updated. A and C are difficult but possible, and there is no facility as described in D.

Choose the appropriate technology to resolve specified problems. Technology options include:

- WWW service
- FTP service
- Microsoft Transaction Server
- Microsoft SMTP Service
- Microsoft NNTP Service
- Microsoft Index Server
- Microsoft Certificate Server

Internet servers provide a combination of services that in sum create a total Internet environment for users. Different environments require different services, and not all services are necessary in all environments. In fact, WWW service is the only "universal" service that appears on most Internet servers. Other peripheral services like FTP,

Mail, and News are niche services that are used on relatively few servers. IIS4 provides all these and other services so you can customize your Internet server to fit your needs exactly.

Critical Information

Understanding the functionality of the different IIS4 components is critical to your success, not only for this objective but for the entire exam. You must understand the functionality of all of the major services of IIS4 if you expect to pass the exam.

WWW Service

World Wide Web service is the premier content formatting service on the Internet—it is single-handedly responsible for the explosion in Internet services, and its presence is so widespread that the term Internet is often confused with the WWW service alone. If you are installing IIS, you're installing it to serve Web pages in addition to whatever else you might be doing.

WWW service allows you to post text documents with codes embedded to change the text's on-screen appearance, to display graphical files, and to link to other text documents. Enhancements to this basic functionality allow scripts, interpreted languages, and compiled code to be embedded in Web pages, and provide a method to return data from clients to the Web server. These enhancements provide a truly interactive multimedia experience. WWW service and its various enhancements can be used to create any client-side interface to a service. For this reason, it's frequently the only service you'll need to provide.

SEE ALSO Chapter 7, "Managing World Wide Web Sites," in *MCSE: Internet Information Server 4 Study Guide* provides additional information about the WWW service.

FTP Service

File Transfer Protocol provides an interface through which files can be copied between Internet hosts. FTP provides a login facility and a method to browse directories and either download or upload files. FTP is commonly used whenever a reliable and efficient means to transfer files across the Internet is needed.

SEE ALSO   Chapter 8, "FTP, Mail, and News," in *MCSE: Internet Information Server 4 Study Guide* provides additional information about the FTP service.

Microsoft Transaction Server

Microsoft Transaction Server provides a way to bundle together any number of operations into a single atomic transaction which, once initiated, will either succeed in its entirety or fail without partially succeeding. This functionality is critical for many financial business activities that occur on the Internet. For example, imagine you are transferring money between bank accounts via your Web browser. Imagine that your computer crashes just after the command to subtract money from your checking account is issued, but before the command to add money to your savings account occurs. What happens? Your money is simply lost. With transactions, the entire transaction will succeed or it will fail—either is okay, because you won't lose your money in either case.

TIP   Don't blow a brain cell trying to figure out exactly what Transaction Server does. It's a system integration package that very few people who set up Web sites will ever use, because it requires custom written software. The MCSE exam does not expect you to understand Transaction Server.

Microsoft SMTP Service

The SMTP Service supplied with IIS4 allows you to add "send mail" functionality to your Web sites. The service does not come with any simple way for multiple users to retrieve mail or with a POP service, so it's not very useful as a mail receiver. The primary purpose for this service is to allow you to create forms for customer support and user response that can be mailed to other addresses from your Web server.

Microsoft NNTP Service

The Microsoft NNTP service allows you to create bulletin boards of topical discussion threads. This could be used for customer support or as a public form of e-mail inside your company.

Microsoft Index Server

Microsoft Index Server is used to provide "search engine" functionality for your Web sites. Index Server scans all the Web pages (and any other documents for which a scanning filter exists) on your server and creates a massive index of every word in every document. When a user enters a search phrase, all documents that contain all the words listed in the search phrase are returned in a new Web document. The user can then click on the hyperlink for each matching document to view it directly. Index Server provides a quick way for users to find specific information on your site.

SEE ALSO   Chapter 14, "Index Server," in *MCSE: Internet Information Server 4 Study Guide* goes into this topic in depth.

Microsoft Certificate Server

Secure Socket Layer (the protocol used to secure data exchanges between Web browsers and Web servers) uses digital files called keys to encrypt data. Before you can require SSL communications for a directory, therefore, you must create keys for your Web site. But before you can install keys into your Web site you have to have them certified with a certificate authority.

Certificates and certificate authorities assure Web users that your Web site is registered with a responsible organization and is safe to visit. A certificate is a message from that responsible organization (the certificate authority) that identifies your server and resides on your server. Your server can give that message to Web browsers to prove its identity.

Certificate Server allows you to act as your own certificate authority for the purpose of generating SSL keys. Microsoft IIS requires a certificate from a certificate authority before you can require SSL on a directory. If you act as your own certificate authority, however, visitors to your Web site do not get the benefit of knowing that your Web site credentials have been scrutinized by a respected third party (unless you join your Certificate Server to a Certificate Authority Hierarchy). Certificate Authorities matter only if your users care that someone other than yourself has generated your SSL certificate.

Exam Essentials

There's only one thing you need to understand for this objective: Everything. Make sure you know what the various components of IIS4 do, why you would use them, and when it's appropriate to install them.

Know the functions of the various services and applications that compose Internet Information Server 4.

- **WWW service** serves the HTTP protocol, which is used to transfer HTML-formatted text documents like Web pages.

- **FTP service** provides a protocol for the transfer of files between hosts over TCP/IP.

- **Transaction Server** provides a method to encapsulate a number of different discrete operations into one operation that must either succeed or fail as a single unit.

- **SMTP Service** allows your Web server to operate as an Internet mail host for the purpose of generating or receiving mail. SMTP does not provide the functionality required for individual mailboxes, which is provided by the POP protocol (not included with IIS4).

- **NNTP Service** allows your server to act as a news host, to provide a forum for public topical discussions.

- **Index Server** will scan every Web document (or other documents having Index Server filters) on your site and add them to a central catalog which can be searched by keyword to find specific pages of interest.

- **Certificate Server** allows you to create your own SSL certificates so you don't have to use an established certificate authority.

Key Terms and Concepts

Certificates: These are digital files that are practically impossible to forge. These files are used to validate the identity of a service provider when generating keys.

File Transfer Protocol (FTP):   A service used to transmit files over TCP/IP networks like the Internet.

Hypertext Transfer Protocol (HTTP):   A service used to transmit HTML (Hypertext Markup Language) encoded text files (and other multimedia content) over the Internet.

Keys: Digital files used as mathematical operators in the encryption process. The longer a key is, the stronger the encryption and the more difficult it is to crack.

Net News Transfer Protocol (NNTP):   A service used to browse discussion groups by topic, to read individual messages in a topic, and to post responses.

Secure Socket Layer (SSL):   A service used to encrypt data on the transmit end of a TCP stream and decrypt the data on the receive end. It provides a transparent method to secure communications between two-end systems.

Simple Mail Transfer Protocol (SMTP):   A service used to exchange addressed text messages between Internet hosts. It is the transfer protocol for Internet e-mail systems.

Sample Questions

1. You want to provide a technical support Web site that offers a list of frequently asked questions, bulletins of problems your technicians have already solved indexed by topic, and a way for users to ask questions privately. Which services should you install?

   A. NNTP, Certificate Server, FTP

   B. WWW, NNTP, SMTP

   C. WWW, Certificate Server, SMTP

   D. WWW, Index Server, SMTP

   Answer: B. Web service for frequently asked questions, NNTP for a bulletin board, and SMTP for e-mail service.

2. You want to open an Internet shopping service that locates the best price for consumer items and purchases it on behalf of the consumer. You need to provide a graphical front end and an order-taking service that will e-mail you with the customer's requirements and credit card number. You want to set up the service without outside assistance. Which services should you install?

   A. NNTP, Certificate Server, FTP

   B. WWW, NNTP, SMTP

   C. WWW, Certificate Server, SMTP

   D. WWW, Index Server, SMTP

   Answer: C. Web services for the front end, Certificate Server to allow the use of SSL keys, and SMTP for e-mail service.

3. You've created an online law library that contains the text of all criminal and civil judgments available from public sources since 1776 (whew!). You want your clients to be able to search the database any way they can think of. You also want the service to be able to e-mail content back to the client in addition to providing it on screen. What services should you install?

   A. NNTP, Certificate Server, FTP

   B. WWW, NNTP, SMTP

C. WWW, Certificate Server, SMTP

D. WWW, Index Server, SMTP

Answer: D. Web services for on-screen viewing, Index Server for searching, and SMTP to e-mail content.

CHAPTER

2

Installation and Configuration

Microsoft Exam Objectives Covered in This Chapter:

▶ **Install IIS. Tasks include:** *(pages 34 – 39)*
- Configuring a Microsoft Windows NT Server 4.0 computer for the installation of IIS
- Identifying differences to a Windows NT Server 4.0 computer made by the installation of IIS

▶ **Configure IIS to support the FTP service. Tasks include:** *(pages 39 – 47)*
- Setting bandwidth and user connections
- Setting user logon requirements and authentication requirements
- Modifying port settings
- Setting directory listing style
- Configuring virtual directories and servers

▶ **Configure IIS to support the WWW service. Tasks include:** *(pages 48 – 62)*
- Setting bandwidth and user connections
- Setting user logon requirements and authentication requirements
- Modifying port settings
- Setting default pages
- Setting HTTP 1.1 host header names to host multiple Web sites
- Enabling HTTP Keep-Alives

▶ **Configure and save consoles by using Microsoft Management Console.** *(pages 63 – 69)*

▶ **Verify server settings by accessing the metabase.** *(pages 70 – 72)*

▶ **Choose the appropriate administration method.** *(pages 72 – 75)*

▶ **Install and configure Certificate Server.** *(pages 75 – 78)*

▶ **Install and configure Microsoft SMTP Service.** *(pages 79 – 82)*

▶ **Install and configure Microsoft NNTP Service.** *(pages 83 – 86)*

▶ **Customize the installation of Microsoft Site Server Express Content Analyzer.** *(pages 87 – 90)*

▶ **Customize the installation of Microsoft Site Server Express Usage Import and Report Writer.** *(pages 91 – 95)*

T his chapter is all about installing IIS correctly to serve the protocols you need for your site. The chapter provides an outline for installing the various protocols and understanding the choices you'll need to make while installing. Determining which protocols to install is the purpose of Chapter 1.

This chapter covers the installation and configuration of:

- FTP service

- WWW service

- Microsoft Management Console

- Microsoft Certificate Server

- Microsoft SMTP Service

- Microsoft NNTP Service

- Microsoft Site Server Express Content Analyzer

- Microsoft Site Server Express with Report Writer

Procedures to install the most important features of these services are covered in the objectives that follow.

SEE ALSO Chapters 2 ("Planning Your Site") and 3 ("Installing Internet Information Server 4") in *MCSE: Internet Information Server 4 Study Guide* by Matthew Strebe and Charles Perkins (Sybex, 1998) amplify the information presented in this chapter.

Install IIS. Tasks include:

- Configuring a Microsoft Windows NT Server 4.0 computer for the installation of IIS
- Identifying differences to a Windows NT Server 4.0 computer made by the installation of IIS

Installing Internet Information Server is easy; understanding the services provided by each of the available options isn't necessarily so easy. This section shows you the basic installation process, explains the changes made to your system by IIS, and sets the stage for the installation of the remaining services that come with the Option Pack for NT Server 4 or NT Server 5.

Critical Information

IIS4 requires the following hardware and preinstalled software:

- At least an Intel Pentium 90MHz with 32MB RAM or a DEC Alpha 200MHz with 64MB RAM and 200MB available hard disk space
- Microsoft Windows NT Server 4
- NT4 Service Pack 3
- Internet Explorer 4

You will also need to obtain the Option Pack for Windows NT Server 4 if your copy of Windows NT didn't come with it. You can download or order the CD-ROM for the Option Pack, Internet Explorer, or Service Pack 3 from Microsoft at www.microsoft.com.

During the installation process, you'll notice a number of components that aren't covered anywhere in this book. That's because these components are for esoteric or very specific applications that are outside the scope of normal Internet site administration. These tools are not critical for IIS administration or exam purposes, but you may use them if you need to develop transaction-based applications for Internet Information Server. Most users will never use the services that are not covered in this volume.

SEE ALSO   Check the online documentation for information about these additional components.

Necessary Procedures

The following two procedures show you how to install the components you need to know about for the Internet Information Server 4 exam and help you understand what changes the installation makes to your server.

Configuring a Microsoft Windows NT Server 4.0 Computer for the Installation of IIS

This procedure will install the default components necessary to completely understand the exam objectives and successfully complete the test. As you go through this process, watch the dialog boxes that the wizard raises to see the options.

TIP   You'll need to specify an administration account with administrator equivalence during the IIS4 setup process. Consider setting up a new administrative account used only for IIS remote administration, so that in the unlikely event your IIS administrative account is compromised, the remainder of your network remains secure.

---

1. Prepare a server by installing Windows NT Server 4, Service Pack 3, and Internet Explorer 4.01.

2. Insert the Option Pack CD-ROM or download the Option Pack from Microsoft's Web site.

3. Browse to the CD-ROM or the location where you've stored the Option Pack and double-click the setup icon.

4. (If upgrading, click OK to acknowledge that Gopher is no longer supported.) Click Next.

5. Click Accept to agree to the end-user licensing agreement.

6. Click Custom (or Upgrade Plus if upgrading) for a custom installation.

7. Check Certificate Server.

8. Double-click Internet Information Server.

9. Check NNTP Service, and ensure SMTP Service is checked.

10. Check World Wide Web Sample Site if it's not already checked and then click OK. This sample site will assist you in sorting out the specific behaviors of IIS, so it's a good idea to install it unless you already know everything you need to know about IIS.

11. Check Index Server if it's not already checked.

12. Check Microsoft Site Server Express if it's not already checked and then click Next.

13. Accept the default file locations and click Next. If the default volume does not have enough room for the IIS site files, select one that does.

14. Accept the default MTS location and click Next.

15. Select Remote.

16. Enter the name of the Administrator or a member of the Administrators group.

17. Enter the password for this account in both the Password and Confirm input boxes and then click Next.

18. Click Next to accept the default Index Server Catalog directory.

19. Click Next to accept the default mail root directory.

20. Click Next to accept the default NNTP root directory.

21. Enter **C:\certserver** (or another location if desired) in the Configuration Data Storage Locations shared directory input box, then click Next and click OK to create the directory.

22. Click OK to create the **%systemroot%\System32\CertLog** directory.

23. Fill out the certificate authority input boxes as appropriate for your organization, then click Next.

24. Click Finish and then click Yes to restart your computer.

Identifying Differences to a Windows NT Server 4.0 Computer Made by the Installation of IIS

The following changes are made to a running Windows NT Server when you install Internet Information Server 4 from the Option Pack as described in the previous section:

1. The Windows NT 4.0 Option Pack elements are added to the Start ➤ Programs menu, including shortcuts to all the Option Pack administration tools.

2. Directories for components selected during installation are created and populated with the default files for each service installed.

3. The following additional services are installed when you follow the installation procedure in the previous section:

   - Certificate Authority
   - Content Index (Index Server)
   - FTP Publishing Service
   - IIS Admin Service
   - Microsoft NNTP Service
   - Microsoft SMTP Service
   - Protected Storage
   - RADIUS Server/Proxy
   - World Wide Web Publishing Service

4. Several keys are added to the registry and some existing keys are modified. You do not need to understand the purpose or location of these keys to administer IIS or to successfully complete the exam.

5. Two user accounts are created for administrative purposes: the IUSR_ *computername* account used to apply NTFS security to anonymous Internet browsers and the IWAM_*computername* account used to control permissions for Web applications.

Exam Essentials

There's one basic thing you need to know for this objective:

Know how to install Internet Information Server 4.   Installing Internet Information Server 4 is as easy as running an installation wizard and selecting the components you need for your site.

Key Terms and Concepts

Option Pack: A suite of tools to enhance the Internet service functionality of Windows NT Server. You may not need to install an option pack if you don't need the functionality provided for your server.

Service Pack: A package of bug fixes and minor updates issued to strengthen the reliability and security of Windows NT. Service packs should be installed shortly after their release on all Windows NT Server computers.

Sample Questions

1. You have installed Windows NT Server 4, Service Pack 3, and Internet Explorer 4.01 on a 100MHz Intel Pentium computer with 24MB of RAM and a 1.0GB hard-disk drive. You are informed that Microsoft does not suggest installing Option Pack for NT Server 4 on this system. Why?

   A. You must install IIS3.

B. You must install a larger hard disk.

C. You need to install more RAM.

D. Your microprocessor is not powerful enough.

Answer: C. Microsoft does not recommend running IIS4 on Intel systems with less than 32MB of RAM.

2. You have installed Windows NT Server 4 and Service Pack 3 on a 333MHz Intel Pentium II computer with 128MB of RAM and a 6.0GB hard disk drive. The installation wizard will not run. Why?

A. You must install IIS3.

B. You must install Internet Explorer 4.01.

C. You need to install more RAM.

D. Your microprocessor is not powerful enough.

Answer: B. You must have Internet Explorer 4.01 or higher installed prior to installing Internet Information Server.

Configure IIS to support the FTP service. Tasks include:

- Setting bandwidth and user connections
- Setting user logon requirements and authentication requirements
- Modifying port settings
- Setting directory listing style
- Configuring virtual directories and servers

Critical Information

FTP provides a simple protocol for transferring files over TCP/IP networks like the Internet. Configuring the FTP service in IIS4 is easy.

The Microsoft Management Console does a good job of centralizing and simplifying the administrative functions required for FTP service.

IIS4 creates the default FTP site on port 21 during the installation process. Often, this site will serve your needs perfectly. To use it you need only modify the service parameters for the default FTP site in the Microsoft Management Console to suit your requirements and store your files in the default directory C:\Inetpub\ftproot (or other directory as specified during the installation process).

If you intend to serve more than one FTP site, you should configure the FTP Master Properties in the Microsoft Management Console to suit the majority of your needs. New sites created will automatically inherit those settings, so you'll only need to change them when you want the settings for a specific FTP service to be different.

Necessary Procedures

The following procedures will walk you through the steps required to create an FTP site and change all the useful settings for it. For all procedures, you should start by having the Microsoft Management Console open and displaying the IIS4 host:

1. Select Start ➣ Programs ➣ Windows NT Server 4.0 Option Pack ➣ Microsoft Internet Information Server ➣ Internet Service Manager.

2. Click Close to dismiss the Tip of the Day if it comes up.

3. Expand by double-clicking the Internet Information Server snap-in.

4. Expand the local host computer.

TIP Instead of right-clicking in the procedures below, you can always select a component and then click the Action toolbar button. This is important to remember while taking the exam because many computers used in testing centers are old and may not correctly respond to right-clicking.

Create FTP Site

Creating an FTP site is simple in IIS4. Additional FTP sites are sometimes referred to as "virtual servers" in Microsoft documentation.

1. Right-click the local host and select New ➤ FTP Site.

2. Enter a descriptive name for the site and click Next.

3. Select the IP address you want this FTP site to respond to if different from the default of All Unassigned. Enter the port you want this site to respond to if different from the default of 21. Click Next.

4. Enter the path to the directory containing the files you wish to serve. Click the Browse button to browse to it if desired. If you intend to serve a new directory, you must create the directory before you can enter its name here. Click Next.

5. Check Read Access and Write Access if desired, then click Finish. You've now created an FTP site.

6. Right-click the new site in the scope pane and select Start.

TIP   If you get a message stating that the new site could not be started because it is not correctly configured, you've already got an FTP site or other Internet service running on the port you assigned. Stop and disable the other service or select a new port to run your new FTP site on. FTP sites cannot share the same port the way Web sites can, because no host header functionality for FTP exists.

Setting Bandwidth and Limiting User Connections

Limiting the bandwidth used by Web and FTP sites is useful when a server's primary purpose is not Internet service and you don't want to flood your Internet connection with service traffic, or in situations where you have to pay for bandwidth and you'd like to limit your costs. For FTP sites, it is not possible to limit bandwidth on a per-site or per-service basis, but you can use this procedure to limit the band-width of all WWW and FTP services:

1. Right-click on your local host server and select Properties.

2. Enter the maximum number of kilobytes per second you want for all combined FTP and WWW traffic.

3. Click OK.

Limiting the number of users of an FTP site is useful when providing FTP service is not the primary function of a server and you don't want FTP use to bog down other services. Limiting users does not limit the amount of bandwidth used, but it does limit memory and compute resources and can also supplement security on sites where more than one or two users is never appropriate. Use the following procedure to limit the simultaneous number of users for a site:

1. Right-click the FTP site and select Properties.

2. Select the FTP site tab.

3. Select Limited To and enter 10 in the input box.

4. Click OK.

Setting User Logon Requirements and Authentication Requirements

Public FTP sites must allow anonymous users to log in. Private sites often don't want anonymous use. You can configure an FTP site to allow either or both. The Allow Only Anonymous Connections setting prevents accounts which may exist on your server (like the Administrator account) from being used over the Internet to gain full control of the site. Use the following procedure to allow or disallow anonymous access to a site and to select which users will be allowed to log into the site via FTP:

1. Right-click the FTP site and select Properties.

2. Select the Security Accounts tab.

3. Check the Allow Anonymous Connection box if you wish to allow public access to the site, otherwise clear the box. Check the Allow Only Anonymous Connections if you wish to ensure passwords are never sent over the network to access this site.

4. Click Add to add specific user accounts or groups to the FTP Site Operators list.

5. Select the account you wish to allow access and click Add.

6. Click OK.

7. Click OK.

Modifying Port Settings

You may want to host multiple FTP sites on your server, or connect certain sites to specific network interfaces on your server—for example, to have one site for internal users and one site for external users. By using a separate IP address for each site, you can have two FTP sites on the same port (e.g., on port 21) if the server has more than one IP address bound to its network interface. Use this procedure to change the TCP/IP properties of your FTP site:

1. Right-click the FTP site and select Properties.

2. Select the FTP Site tab.

3. Enter the port you want this site to respond to in the TCP Port input box.

4. Change the IP address setting as necessary.

5. Click OK.

Setting Directory Listing Style

Use this procedure to change the default MS-DOS directory listing style to the more compatible UNIX directory listing style. The MS-DOS listing style will not work with most FTP client programs because it presents an incompatible directory listing style that these tools cannot parse.

1. Right-click the FTP site and select Properties.

2. Select the Home Directory tab.

3. Select the UNIX listing style for compatibility with all GUI-based FTP utilities.

4. Click OK.

Configuring Virtual Directories and Servers

Virtual directories allow you to serve files that exist in locations outside the ftproot directory structure. The actual location of a virtual directory may be anywhere on your network. (Creating virtual servers is covered under the Create FTP site procedure, above.) Use the following procedure to create FTP virtual directories:

1. Right-click the FTP site and select New ➤ Virtual Directory.

2. Type the name for this directory (for example, **public**) as you want it to show in the FTP directory structure, and press Enter to proceed to the next pane.

3. Enter the local directory pathname or the UNC pathname to the share and the directory you want the virtual directory to point to. You may click the Browse button to browse the local machine or the Network Neighborhood. Click Next when finished.

4. Enter a username and password to be used as credentials to access this site if the directory exists on another computer. You may use the IUSR_*computername* account, but you'll have to set the password here to authorize entry to the site. Click Next. Re-enter the password to confirm and click OK.

5. Check to allow Read Access and Write Access as desired.

6. Click Finish.

You can right-click an FTP virtual directory and select Properties to modify any of these parameters at a later time.

TIP If you see a red stop sign that says Error in the Scope Pane after you create an FTP virtual root, you most likely incorrectly entered the account name or password for the connecting account.

Exam Essentials

You must be very familiar with the following information to pass the Microsoft exam for IIS4:

Know your way around the Microsoft Management Console as it applies to FTP. This is the most important aspect of training for the exam, as the exam simulator is the same as the Microsoft Management Console and you are required to perform procedures for many tasks similar to those presented here. Remember that as an alternative to right-clicking you can always use the Action button in the toolbar after selecting a component, because many exam computers are old and slow and may not respond to right-clicking as quickly as you are used to on your own computer.

Know how to create new FTP sites. There are two ways to create new FTP sites: Right-click your local host and select New ➤ FTP Site or right-click any FTP site and select New ➤ Site.

Know that virtual servers are now synonymous with sites. Don't be confused by the term "virtual server." It just refers to what is now called a site.

Know how to change FTP service parameters. Be able to change all the FTP service parameters like ports, security accounts, sign-on messages, and so forth for both the Master service properties and for individual sites.

Know how to limit IIS bandwidth. The Microsoft objectives are written in a way that implies that bandwidth can be limited on a per-site or per-service basis for FTP. They cannot—only the WWW service allows limiting bandwidth on a per-site basis. You can limit the bandwidth of all FTP and WWW services combined in the Master Properties dialog box.

Key Terms and Concepts

Directory listing style: The manner in which FTP information is transmitted back to an FTP client. FTP clients that are not text-based are not compatible with the MS-DOS directory listing style.

FTP site (FTP virtual server) : A collection of related files stored in a directory tree that is served by the Microsoft FTP service on a specific TCP/IP address and port number with similar security requirements. One server may have multiple FTP sites, but they must all be on unique TCP ports.

Port: A TCP/IP parameter that specifies which communication stream (or conversation) a packet belongs to. Services listen for connections on specific well-known ports when they provide a public service like FTP or WWW service.

Virtual directory: An alias to a directory inside an FTP site that resides somewhere other than in the FTP site directory tree—for example, on another volume or another computer. Some security settings can be applied differently to virtual directories than they are applied to the FTP site as a whole.

Sample Questions

1. Create an FTP virtual directory called results with the physical path d:\results with read/write access in an FTP site from a running MMC console. Choose the appropriate steps:

   A. Right-click the FTP site, select New ➤ Site, type **results** in the site description input box, click Next, type **d:\results** in the Path input box, check Allow Read Access, check Allow Write Access, click Finish.

   B. Right-click the FTP site, select New ➤ Virtual Directory, type **results** in the Alias input box, type **d:\results** in the Path input box, check Allow Read Access, check Allow Write Access, click Finish.

C. Right-click the host computer, select New ➤ FTP Site, type **results** in the site description input box, click Next, type **d:\results** in the Path input box, check Allow Read Access, check Allow Write Access, click Finish.

D. Right-click the FTP site, select New ➤ Virtual Directory, type **results** in the Alias input box, type **d:\results** in the Path input box, click Finish.

Answer: B. A and C create a new FTP site, D does not implement access permissions correctly.

2. Change an FTP service port to port 2121 to prevent conflicts with a proxy running on the same machine. Choose the correct sequence:

A. Right-click the FTP site, select Properties, enter **2121** in the IP Address input box, click OK.

B. Right-click the FTP site, select Properties, enter **2121** in the Port input box, click OK.

C. Right-click the local host, select FTP Service in the Master Properties input box, enter **2121** in the Port input box, click OK.

D. Right-click the FTP site, select TCP/IP, enter **2121** in the Port input box, click OK.

Answer: B. The other options don't work.

3. Since you've placed a patch for your software product on your FTP server, users have complained of slow Web access. You have only one 128Kbps connection to the Internet, which is shared by your entire company. Your Web and FTP sites are located on the same machine. What is the simplest way to solve this problem?

A. Remove the patch and mail it to customers on floppy disk.

B. Put your FTP site on a different server.

C. Limit the number of simultaneous FTP connections.

D. Enable bandwidth throttling.

Answer: C. A is not convenient for anyone, B will make no difference because both servers are behind the same slow pipe (the server is not the bottleneck), and D throttles all services, not just FTP.

Configure IIS to support the WWW service. Tasks include:

- Setting bandwidth and user connections
- Setting user logon requirements and authentication requirements
- Modifying port settings
- Setting default pages
- Setting HTTP 1.1 host header names to host multiple Web sites
- Enabling HTTP Keep-Alives

The WWW Service is the flagship of IIS. It is the most complex service and the most important, as it forms the backbone of even the simplest Internet sites. The complexity is easy to manage with the Microsoft Management Console, however—the skills you've already practiced for FTP are nearly identical to those needed to administer WWW sites, with just a few more settings thrown in for advanced features like host headers.

The information presented in this section is perhaps the most important information you'll need to know for the test, because it provides the answers to many exam questions. Be sure you understand everything in this section completely. If anything remains unclear to you when you've read through it a few times and practiced the necessary procedures, refer to other sources for additional clarification.

SEE ALSO Chapter 7 of *MCSE: Internet Information Server 4 Study Guide* covers this information in much greater detail.

Critical Information

The WWW service serves documents in specially formatted text called Hypertext Markup Language (HTML) to clients called Web browsers, which can display the text and images embedded in the document. HTML is transmitted using the TCP/IP-based Hypertext Transfer Protocol (HTTP).

HTML documents are collected into related sets of files called Web sites. Web sites can be individually secured through both IIS security settings and NTFS security to provide different methods of user authentication and different levels of access per user. You can also change convenience and performance features of the various Web sites on your server to most efficiently handle their particular traffic requirements. Most per-site settings can also be set globally for all sites through the WWW Master Properties dialog box.

Web browsers select a specific Web site on an Internet server by one of three methods:

- **By unique IP address.** Each network adapter can respond to multiple IP addresses, and a Web site can be assigned to a specific IP address. This is the most compatible method of hosting multiple Web sites because it works with older browsers that support only the HTTP 1.0 specification. However, since a central authority parcels out Internet IP addresses, more than one may not be available. Use unique IP addresses when multiple IP addresses are available and when you must support legacy Web browsers.

- **By unique TCP port** on the same IP address. Each Web site can be set to respond to a different TCP port. However, since anonymous browsers expect Web sites to respond to port 80, most users may have a difficult time finding sites on other ports. This method also works with HTTP 1.0 browsers. Avoid using unique TCP ports unless no other method of Web site identification is available.

- **By the host header** on the same TCP port and IP address. Each Web site can register the host headers (domain names) to which it will respond. HTTP 1.1 clients transmit a host header to the server when they connect, by which the correct site can be identified without a unique TCP port or IP address. This method is the easiest to implement and the most transparent to users, but it only works with HTTP 1.1–compatible browsers. Use host headers whenever you can rely upon clients to use HTTP 1.1–compatible Web browsers. Figure 2.1 shows various host headers assigned to a Web site.

FIGURE 2.1: Multiple host headers for a single Web site

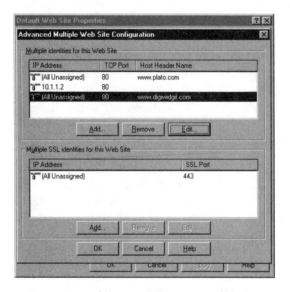

You can individually control the performance features of the various Web sites on your server using the Performance tab of each Web site's Properties dialog box. Low-level site performance parameters are all configured using the Web site tuning slider, which allows you to set performance characteristics for low-, medium-, and high-traffic sites. You can also enable bandwidth throttling to limit the load this site will be allowed to place on your network connections. This is useful when limited bandwidth is available and you don't want certain sites to "flood the pipe." HTTP Keep-Alives can be enabled for sites where performance is critical. HTTP Keep-Alives hold the TCP connection open between requests so that the user doesn't have to wait to reestablish the connection each time a request is made. Unfortunately, there's no way for the browser to inform the server when it actually leaves, so each connection will always remain open for the timeout period when the browser leaves. This is of no consequence except on the most heavily loaded servers.

Authentication is controlled on a per-site basis. Through the Directory Security tab of the Web site Properties window, each Web site can be individually configured to allow one of the following:

- **Anonymous Access,** which allows users to log in without providing an identity. The server automatically uses the account specified in the Directory Security tab to control NTFS security, which by default is the IUSR_*computername* account. If anonymous access is allowed, it is automatically used by the Web browser—a user cannot override anonymous access and provide logon credentials unless the Web site requires them for access.

- **Basic Authentication,** which is the most compatible and widely used method of authentication. Whenever anonymous access is disabled or the NTFS security on a file or directory prevents access, a logon dialog box is displayed. The username and password are transmitted non-securely to the Web browser and the user is logged in using those credentials.

- **Windows NT Challenge/Response authentication,** which is compatible with Internet Explorer only. Whenever anonymous access is disabled or the NTFS security on a file or directory prevents access, the Web browser will automatically transmit a one-way encrypted hash of the account credentials the user used to log onto their local network. If a matching account exists on the Web server, the user will be logged in automatically without raising a logon dialog box. Otherwise, a logon dialog box will pop up on the Web browser and the user must enter a valid account name and password to gain access to the site.

The functionality of a Web site can be enhanced using ISAPI filters. ISAPI filters are compiled code segments specifically written to enhance the functionality of IIS by modifying data as it flows between the server and the client. For example, a simple ISAPI filter could be used to change all the characters in a Web site to upper case, if you had some reason to do that. When a Web site is transmitted to a client, IIS sends the HTML document to each ISAPI filter in succession for processing. Those ISAPI filters can change the document in any conceivable way. For example, the Active Server Pages ISAPI filter actually interprets programming codes embedded in the HTML document to produce entirely new HTML pages as the pages pass through to the client. You can add, remove, and change the order of ISAPI filters on a global or per-site basis using the ISAPI Filters tab of the site Properties dialog box.

Necessary Procedures

The exercises in this section assume that you have the Microsoft Management Console running and the IIS snap-in expanded. Use the following procedure to begin:

1. Select Start ➤ Programs ➤ Windows NT Server 4.0 Option Pack ➤ Microsoft Internet Information Server ➤ Internet Service Manager.

2. Click Close to dismiss the Tip of the Day if it comes up.

3. Expand by double-clicking the Internet Information Server snap-in.

4. Expand the local host computer.

Creating WWW Sites

Although this procedure is not listed as a task in the Microsoft objectives, it is crucial that you know how to create a Web site for the exam. It also provides a good working site where you can test other necessary procedures without modifying any of your existing Web sites. Use the following procedure to create a Web site:

1. Right-click the local host and select New ➤ Web Site or right-click on any existing Web site and select New ➤ Site.

2. Type a description (for example, **test**) for the Web site and press Enter.

3. Select the IP address to which this site will respond, or accept the default of All Unassigned if you will not be using distinct IP addresses to identify sites.

4. Enter the port to which this site will respond, or accept the default of 80 if you will not be using distinct TCP ports to identify sites. Click Next.

5. Enter the path to the home directory for this site or click Browse to browse to it. The directory must already exist.

6. Check Allow Anonymous Access for this site if you do not wish to require logon authentication for the default Web page. (Pages inside the site can require logon authentication through NTFS security.) Clear this checkbox if the site will require logon authentication to access the default Web page.

7. Set the IIS service security settings as necessary to secure this site. For most simple sites, Read and Script permissions are sufficient. For ISAPI Web applications (not filters), allow Execute permission. For HTTP posting, allow Write Access. If you want users to be able to list directories, allow Directory Browsing.

8. Click Finish.

9. Right-click the Web site and select Start.

If you get an error message stating that the Web site could not be started because it is incorrectly configured, you will need to establish a host header to uniquely identify the site because another site already exists on the same TCP port and IP address. Proceed to the next exercise to establish a host header for this site.

Setting HTTP 1.1 Host Header Names to Host Multiple Web Sites

If your Web service is set up in the default state, you will have gotten an error while trying to start the Web site created in the previous procedure. This happens because IIS will not start a Web site with an identity that conflicts with another site. Since neither the IP address nor the TCP port provides a different identity for this site, you must use host headers to make it unique. Use the following procedure to enable host headers:

1. Right-click the Web site and select Properties.

2. Select the Web Site tab.

3. Click the Web Site Identification Advanced button.

4. Click Add.

5. Select All Unassigned in the IP Address pick box.

6. Enter 80 in the TCP port input box.

7. Enter the DNS name assigned to this Web site in the Host Header Name input box (for example, webtest.footest.com).

8. Click OK.

9. Click OK.

10. Click OK.

11. Right-click the Web site and select Start.

TIP   You can have more than one host header for a Web site!

You can test host header functionality before you actually assign DNS names to your servers by using the HOSTS file on your Web server. Use the following procedure to test host header functionality:

1. Select Start ➤ Programs ➤ Accessories ➤ Notepad.

2. Select File ➤ Open.

3. Browse to c:\winnt\system32\drivers\etc\ and open the HOSTS file. There is no .txt extension to this file.

4. Move the cursor to the bottom line of this file. It should be directly below the last text entry of the file.

5. Enter the following text, pressing the Tab key where indicated by {tab} rather than typing out the word "tab": 127.0.0.1{tab} webtest.footest.com.

6. Select File ➤ Exit.

7. Click Yes.

8. Launch Internet Explorer or another HTTP 1.1–compatible Web browser.

9. Enter **webtest.footest.com** in the Address input box.

10. Verify that the correct Web site appears. Close Internet Explorer.

11. Repeat steps 1 through 4.

12. Delete the line containing the text you added in step 5.

13. Repeat steps 6 and 7.

TIP   You can use this handy method to validate any DNS name-based service before you actually assign the DNS names to the server. Just remember to remove entries after you test.

Setting Bandwidth and User Connections

If you serve a wide variety of Web sites, you may want to make sure certain popular Web sites can't bog down your server. This is especially important if you are serving Web sites for other individuals or organizations with content you don't control. Use the following procedure to limit both the number of users and the maximum bandwidth of a specific Web site:

1. Right-click the Web site and select Properties.

2. Select Web Site.

3. Select Limited To in the Connections control group.

4. Enter the maximum number of users in the Limited To input box (for example, **1000**).

5. Select the Performance tab.

6. Check Enable Bandwidth Throttling.

7. Enter the maximum network bandwidth to allow in the input box (for example, 128).

8. Click OK.

Setting User Logon Requirements and Authentication Requirements

This procedure shows you all features of the different authentication methods. You will rarely need to enable all three methods, but they are all enabled here for practice.

1. Right-click a test Web site and select Properties.

2. Select Directory Security.

3. Click the Edit button in the Anonymous Access and Authentication control group.

4. Check Allow Anonymous Access.

5. Click the Edit button in the Anonymous Access control group.

6. Click Browse.

7. Select the IUSR_*computername* account (even if it's already the account listed).

8. Instead of entering the account password, check the Enable Password Synchronization checkbox. Click OK. Click Yes.

9. Check Basic Authentication. Click Yes.

10. Click the Edit button in the Basic Authentication control group.

11. Click Browse. Browse to the domain in which all authentication accounts are stored. Click OK. Click OK.

12. Check Windows NT Challenge/Response authentication.

13. Click OK.

14. Click OK.

Modifying Port Settings

At some time you may develop Web sites you want to operate from different ports. Some sites use unusual ports as a form of security; however, nothing about an unusual port makes a site more secure, because hackers know how to find it anyway. To modify port settings on a site:

1. Right-click a test Web site and select Properties.

2. Select Web Site.

3. Enter a new port to accept connections on in the TCP Port input box (for example, **8081**).

4. Click OK.

5. Launch Internet Explorer.

6. Enter **http://localhost:8081** in the address-input box. Verify that the correct site appears. Close Internet Explorer.

Setting Default Pages

You can assign the name of the default HTML document opened when no file is specified. This is especially helpful when moving a site that was not created for IIS to your Internet server. Use the following procedure to assign a default document name:

1. Right-click a test Web site and select Properties.

2. Select the Documents tab.

3. Click Add.

4. Enter a new default document name (for example, **index.html**) and click OK.

5. With the new name selected, click the up arrow until this default document name is listed above the other default document names.

6. Click OK.

Enabling HTTP Keep-Alives

HTTP Keep-Alives are a performance optimization that makes Web sites more responsive to browsers by keeping the TCP connection open between the browser and the server between requests, thus eliminating the time required to reestablish the connection for each request. Use the following procedure to enable HTTP Keep-Alives:

1. Right-click a test Web site.

2. Select the Performance tab.

3. Check HTTP Keep-Alives Enabled.

4. Click OK.

Exam Essentials

There are a lot of essentials for this objective, because it's one of the most important and most heavily covered on the exam. Make certain you understand the following:

Know how to enable browser login security.   IIS will require a user logon whenever the NTFS access control list (ACL) for a Web page does not include the IUSR_*computername* account or a group in which that account is a member.

Know how to secure a site against use by anonymous browsers and how to change the anonymous user account.   Disable anonymous access by unchecking the Allow Anonymous Access field in the site's Directory Security properties. Enable anonymous access by checking the field and specifying the NTFS account which will be used by anonymous browsers.

Understand and know how to use host headers.   Add a host header for a site by accessing that site's TCP/IP configuration in Home Directory properties, clicking Advanced, and adding the URL to which that site responds.

Understand the different ways sites can be addressed. Web sites can be uniquely addressed on a single server by assigning each its own IP address, by assigning each its own port on a single IP address, or by assigning each its own unique host header on the same port and IP address.

Understand and know how to implement password synchronization. Implement password synchronization through a Web site's Directory Security anonymous user settings dialog box. Password synchronization can also be implemented in the WWW Master Properties dialog box.

Know how to add MIME types. You configure MIME types through the global settings accessed by right-clicking the local server, selecting Properties, and clicking the Add MIME types button. MIME types can only be configured on a global basis.

Know how to add ISAPI filters to Web sites. You can add filters to a specific Web site by accessing the Web site's ISAPI Filters tab, or add filters to all Web sites by accessing the Master Properties ISAPI Filters tab. Filters are processed in the order listed.

Know how to limit connections and bandwidth. Bandwidth for a specific Web site can be limited by checking the Enable Bandwidth Throttling checkbox and entering the kilobytes per second that the site should be limited to. Bandwidth for all WWW and FTP services combined can be limited by changing the bandwidth limitation values on the Master Properties dialog box, accessed by right-clicking the local host and selecting Properties.

Know how to enable HTTP Keep-Alives. Check the HTTP Keep-Alives Enabled checkbox in the Performance tab of a Web site's Properties dialog box to enable this performance feature.

Key Terms and Concepts

Host headers: A new technology introduced in the HTTP 1.1 spec-
ifications which allows Web servers to differentiate Web sites based
on the host text contained in the initial connection negotiation. Prior
to HTTP 1.1, the only way to differentiate Web sites was by TCP
port or IP address. Host headers requires HTTP 1.1–compatible
browsers such as recent versions of Netscape Navigator and Microsoft Internet Explorer.

HTTP Keep-Alives: An optimization which keeps the TCP connection open between a browser and a server between HTTP requests.
Normally, the TCP connection is closed after each request. This optimization allows a server to respond faster to established clients, but
requires more RAM and processor resources from the server.

Hypertext: A specification whereby index links in a text document can be activated in order to move to a different location in the
text document or to another document altogether. Hypertext is the
enabling technology of the World Wide Web.

Hypertext Markup Language (HTML): A set of codes which can
be embedded in normal text documents to delineate headers, text
styles, embedded picture files, and hypertext links.

Hypertext Transfer Protocol (HTTP): A TCP/IP-based protocol
used to negotiate the transfer of hypertext streams between a client
(Web browser) and a server (Web server).

ISAPI filters: Dynamic Link Libraries written to the Internet
Server Application Programming Interface (ISAPI) specification
which process the communication streams as they flow between the
client and the server. ISAPI filters can be used to change Web data
mid-stream in ways that enhance the functionality of IIS—for
example, to implement scripting languages like VBScript or JScript.

Uniform Resource Locator (URL): The textual address of a document on the Web. A URL contains the protocol necessary to
retrieve the document, the DNS name of the server upon which the

document is stored, the path to the document, the document name, and any parameters required for the server to automatically generate the document if it is created dynamically upon request.

Web sites: A collection of related hypertext documents typically addressed from the same root URL and embodying a specific purpose. Web sites are an abstract collection used to apply similar security and administrative settings to a set of HTML documents.

Sample Questions

1. You want to test the new version of your Web site before you replace the older version. The older Web site is set up as the default Web site. All of the internal links in your new Web site are relative paths. You have only one IP address and DNS name established for your computer. What is the easiest way to test your new Web site without interrupting service to your old one, and without requiring changes to the DNS setup?

A. Create a host header for the new site with a different host name.

B. Configure your NT server to respond to a different IP address and then select that as the IP address for the new Web site.

C. Enter a different port number for the new Web site to respond to.

D. Install a second copy of Internet Information Server 4 on the computer; set up the new Web site as the default Web site for the new IIS4 installation.

Answer: C. Host Headers and new IP numbers require updating the DNS configuration or HOSTS file for your network—both of which can cause strange results on active sites. You can only have one copy of IIS4 on your computer—if you try to run the installation again, you will simply be asked if you would like to update or remove your current installation.

2. You have created an intranet Web site just for employees of your company. You want to require that people browsing the Web site have Windows NT accounts on your network. How can you make sure that this is the case? (Choose two answers.)

   A. Enable the Allow Anonymous Authentication option in the Directory Security property tab.

   B. Enable the Basic Authentication option in the Directory Security property tab.

   C. Require Secure Socket Layer connections to the Web site's Home Directory.

   D. Enable the Windows NT Challenge/Response option in the Directory Security property tab.

   Answer: B, D. Anonymous authentication will allow anyone to access your Web site. Secure Socket Layer connections encrypt the communications between the browser and your server but does not authenticate the user. Both Windows NT Challenge/Response and Basic Authentication require that the user present a username and password that belong to a valid account on your network.

3. Accesses to your free software download Web site are swamping your Internet connection and making it difficult for users to access your commercial Web site. You want people to continue to be able to access your free site because it provides excellent advertisement for your commercial site, but you want preference to go to people browsing your commercial site. How can you accomplish this? (Choose two answers.)

   A. Enable HTTP Keep-Alives for the commercial site.

   B. Enable bandwidth throttling for the free site.

   C. Enable bandwidth throttling for the commercial site.

   D. Limit the number of simultaneous connections to the free site.

   Answer: B, D. Throttling the bandwidth to the free site and limiting the number of simultaneous connections to the free site both will reduce the load that site puts on the server; however, limiting the bandwidth is a nicer way to do it.

Configure and save consoles by using Microsoft Management Console.

Microsoft has changed the way IIS is configured in version 4 with a more coherent and easy-to-use tool called the Management Console. Eventually, all Windows NT Server and BackOffice software will use the Management Console to control their functionality. This objective explains the Management Console basics you need to understand for both real-world administration and the exam. You've already become familiar with the Management Console if you've read this chapter from the beginning and performed the exercises in the FTP and WWW service sections.

Critical Information

The Microsoft Management Console (MMC) is a single application used to control the settings of multiple services. Currently, all IIS settings can be controlled through the MMC. Future versions of Windows NT (starting with version 5) will use the MMC to replace current administrative tools like the User Manager for Domains and the Server Manager. For this reason, time spent learning the MMC now with IIS4 is especially well spent.

How can one tool be so flexible as to manage services that aren't even available yet? Through extensions called snap-ins. The MMC controls nothing by itself—every service you want to use the MMC with must provide a special ActiveX control called a snap-in that conforms to the MMC interface specification. Snap-ins can be individually loaded or unloaded from the MMC.

Each snap-in provides a hierarchical view of the settings for whatever services it controls. This display hierarchy is called a namespace. The hierarchy consists first of services which can be controlled. From there, what is displayed is up to the individual snap-in. In the case of

IIS, IIS servers in the network are displayed next, then individual Web, FTP, SMTP, and NNTP sites. Inside each site, the directories contained in that site are generally displayed next. Figure 2.2 shows this hierarchy quite clearly.

FIGURE 2.2: The IIS namespace in the MMC

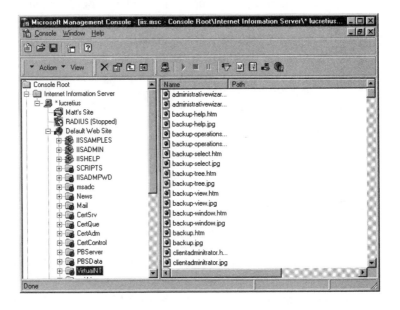

The MMC display is split into two panes. The left pane, called the scope pane, displays the browseable hierarchical namespace. The right pane, called the results pane, contains the contents of the currently selected object in the scope pane. For example, if a Web site is selected in the scope pane, its directories are displayed in the results pane. This is the same concept used by the desktop Explorer to display the hierarchical directory structure of your disk on the left and the contents of the currently selected folder on the right.

MMC Settings File Contents

You can load and save various combinations of snap-in settings in files called consoles. Consoles are simply files that describe a set of MMC settings, such as which snap-ins are loaded and what the scope pane displays. For this reason, console files are quite small (usually less than 10K) and are suitable for e-mailing or otherwise distributing as you please to administrators. You can create new empty console files, and then add snap-ins to them to create custom administrative tools for the various services you wish to control. Currently, snap-ins are available for the following services:

- Internet Information Server

- Index Server

- Transaction Server

You can add any or all of these services to an MMC console by loading the snap-in that controls them. Some snap-ins can be extended to provide functionality beyond their default functionality. The IIS snap-in, for example, can be extended to control the SMTP and NNTP services in addition to the default Web and FTP control it provides.

Currently, console files cannot effectively be locked to limit their administrative functionality. Microsoft has announced that future versions will be secured so that you can create individual console files for users of your network. This allows those users to effectively administer the services under their direct authority without affecting services controlled by others. For example, you can currently create a console that has just the IIS snap-in loaded and which displays a single Web site called HumanResources. You can then provide this console file to the HR director at your company to control the HR Web site. In the future, you'll be able to secure the console file so that the HR director cannot use it to control any other Web sites.

You've already used the MMC in previous sections of this chapter to control the Web and FTP services, so its behavior with services should be quite clear. Loading and saving consoles is quite easy: simply select Console ➤ Save to save a console, Console ➤ Load to load a console, and Console ➤ New to create a new one. The MMC behaves just like any other multiple document interface Windows application.

For each console, you'll use Console ➤ Add/Remove Snap-in to select the snap-ins you want to load. You can extend certain extendable snap-ins by selecting the Extensions tab in the Add/Remove Snap-ins dialog box and then checking those extensions you want loaded.

Necessary Procedures

Creating, saving, and loading MMC consoles is quite easy. Each console is a normal file containing configuration information such as which snap-ins are contained, how windows are laid out, and to what level the hierarchical views are expanded. Use the following procedure to create, save, and reload an MMC console.

1. Select Start ➤ Programs ➤ Windows NT 4.0 Option Pack ➤ Microsoft Internet Information Server ➤ Internet Service Manager.

2. Select Console ➤ New to create a new empty console file.

3. Select Console ➤ Add/Remove Snap-in.

4. Click Add.

5. Double-click Internet Information Server.

6. Click OK.

7. Expand the Internet Information Server snap-in and the server's icon to display the default Web and FTP sites.

8. Select Console ➤ Save.

9. Browse to the desktop (the topmost setting in the directory pick list). This will store the console on the desktop so you can easily launch it from its desktop icon.

10. Enter iis in the File Name input box. The .msc extension will be added automatically.

11. Click the console window Close box.

12. Select Console ➤ Open.

13. Browse to the desktop and select iis.msc.

Exam Essentials

Understand the MMC methodology. The MMC provides a viewer/browser for hierarchical service administration objects called snap-ins. Snap-ins can be individually loaded and configured for different administrative purposes.

Understand the contents of MMC console files. Console files contain sets of settings describing which snap-ins are loaded and how the scope pane and window settings should appear for a specific administrative purpose.

Know how to add and remove snap-ins. Adding and removing snap-ins from a console file is easily accomplished through the Add/Remove Snap-ins dialog box available in the MMC Console menu.

Know how to load and save consoles. Consoles can be easily created, saved, and reloaded using the MMC Console menu. The MMC conforms to the standard Windows multiple document interface.

Know that console files can be distributed easily. Console files are small and contain no data specific to the services controlled by snap-ins. They are easily distributed via e-mail or any other distribution mechanism to assist in the delegation of administrative authority.

Key Terms and Concepts

Console file: A small file containing settings which control the snap-ins to be loaded and the display windows and their contents for an MMC administrative purpose.

Namespace: A hierarchical view of controllable objects, which shows clearly how objects relate to one another. Snap-ins expose their namespace to the MMC, which is used to browse the various controllable objects.

Snap-in: A special ActiveX control that controls a Windows NT service and exposes a namespace that can be controlled by the MMC.

Sample Questions

1. Choose the answer that describes the steps necessary to add the Index Server snap-in to the Microsoft Management Console.

    A. From the MMC, select Console ➢ Add/Remove Snap-in, double-click Index Server, click Finish, and click OK.

    B. From the MMC, select Console ➢ Open, browse to C:\ Inetpup\Snapins, double-click Index Server, click Finish, and click OK.

    C. From the MMC, select Console ➢ Add/Remove Snap-in, click Add, double-click Index Server, click Finish, and click OK.

    D. From the MMC, select Console ➢ Add/Remove Snap-in, Browse to C:\Inetpup\Snapins, double-click Index Server, click Finish, and click OK.

    Answer: C

2. You have a Web hosting company that creates medical directories and indexes them so patients can search for doctors easily. Your Web sites are broken down into various specialties, such as Ophthalmology, Pediatrics, and Internal Medicine. You have a different administrator responsible for each specialty. How can you make Web administration easiest for each administrator?

    A. Create a different IIS admin site for each administrator that will allow them to manage their sites through the HTML Internet Service Managers.

    B. Write scripts to manage sites and require your administrators to learn a scripting language. ˙

C. Bypass administration by using the MDUtil program to directly edit the metabase.

D. Create custom consoles for the administrators; each administrator's console should display only the Web site that that administrator needs to access.

Answer: D. Custom consoles created to solve specific problems make administration easier.

3. You need to delegate responsibility for various Web sites on your IIS-based intranet to departmental representatives in your company.

Proposed Solution: Create a separate MMC console for each departmental representative. Write-protect the .msc files that result to prevent them from being changed.

Required Result: Departmental representatives should be able to administer their own Web sites easily.

Optional Result: Departmental representatives should not be able to administer other Web sites.

Choose the correct answer:

A. The solution fulfills the required result and the optional result.

B. The solution fulfills the required result but not the optional result.

C. The solution does not fulfill the required result but does fulfill the optional result.

D. The solution fulfills neither the required nor the optional result.

Answer: B. Although write-protecting an .msc file will prevent the file from being saved with new snap-ins or settings, it doesn't prevent a user from changing administrative settings while the console is in use.

Verify server settings by accessing the metabase.

You will not directly manipulate the metabase either for the exam or real-world administration purposes. For that reason, this objective is not important—it is a remnant of the beta-test phase of IIS during which IIS settings in the metabase had to be directly manipulated with a command-line utility because the MMC was not yet finished. The command-line utility still ships with IIS, but there's no reason to use it. The metabase is covered here solely for the sake of complete compliance with the Microsoft objectives.

Critical Information

The metabase stores all the IIS settings you can modify with the MMC—for instance, names of Web sites, the ports they run on, the IIS service security settings for the various sites, and any other configurable Web site information. Each time a customer accesses a Web site, IIS accesses the metabase—to determine, for instance, what the security settings for that specific request are before returning it.

The metabase is a speed-optimized registry Microsoft created for IIS because the older method of storing IIS configuration data in the Windows NT registry made IIS too slow to compete with other Web servers. Like the registry, the metabase is a hierarchical database of settings stored as key-value pairs. Unlike the registry, the metabase is optimized for access by IIS directly without going through the operating system services of Windows NT.

Some IIS settings are still stored in the registry for backward compatibility with tools written for IIS, but those settings are only written to the registry for the use of other programs. Whenever IIS checks the value of a setting, the value comes from the metabase.

TIP   The metabase is simply a registry that has been optimized for speed.

Necessary Procedures

Use the following procedure to directly view metabase settings:

1. Select Start ➤ Programs ➤ Command Prompt.

2. Type **cd \winnt\system32.**

3. Type **mdutil enum_all w3svc metadata.txt.**

4. Type **notepad metadata.txt.**

5. Browse through the data displayed in the `metadata.txt` file.

6. Close the notepad.

7. Type **del metadata.txt.**

8. Close the command prompt.

Exam Essentials

This objective is not important to the exam or to real-world administration, because all access to the metabase is performed through the Microsoft Management Console. This objective is actually just a remnant of the beta-test program for IIS4, which required direct manipulation of the metabase because the Management Console was not yet finished.

Key Terms and Concepts

Metabase: A speed-optimized hierarchical database of IIS settings which is similar to the Windows NT Registry.

Sample Questions

You will not see any questions on the exam that concern direct manipulation of the metabase—spend your time studying the Microsoft Management Console, since all metabase settings are configured through it.

Choose the appropriate administration method.

This objective is about determining when to use the MMC to administer IIS and when to use the HTML service managers to do so.

Critical Information

There are two ways to administer IIS: directly, using the MMC and the IIS snap-in, or through the HTML service managers. HTML service managers are provided for the following services:

- IIS (WWW and FTP)
- NNTP
- SMTP
- Index Server

The HTML service managers are organized a little differently than the MMC, but they do a remarkable job of simulating its functionality. You can control nearly every IIS setting with the HTML service managers. Despite this functionality, they're rather clunky and slow compared to the MMC because of the additional processing required to format data for transport over the Internet. Because of this additional overhead, you'll rarely use the HTML service managers except when you need to administer a Web site over the Internet.

The HTML service managers are actually just special Web sites served by IIS that contain Active Server Pages scripts and controls that are capable of changing metabase settings. These pages are all organized under the IISADMIN Web site.

Although it's possible to control remote servers using the MMC, a Windows network must exist between the remote server and the administrative computer. Usually this is prevented by firewalls that are configured to block Windows networking protocols because Windows NT domain security is easily hacked from the Internet. In addition, the bandwidth between the server and the administrative computer must be fairly high because the MMC is not optimized for low speed the way the HTML service managers are. Most IIS servers on the Web have the Server, RPC, and Workstation services disabled to prevent hackers from exploiting security holes in the Windows networking protocols and from attempting to log on as the administrator. Without a regular Windows network connection, you won't be able to use the MMC.

Necessary Procedures

Use the following procedure to launch each of the various HTML management Web sites:

1. Select Start ➤ Programs ➤ Windows NT 4.0 Option Pack ➤ Microsoft Internet Information Server ➤ Internet Service Manager (HTML).

2. Click the + symbol to expand the default Web site.

3. Notice the similarities between the MMC and the administration Web site. The left frame simulates the right-click or action menu in the MMC. The right frame simulates the results pane of the MMC.

4. Close Internet Explorer.

5. Select Start ➤ Programs ➤ Windows NT 4.0 Option Pack ➤ Microsoft Internet Information Server ➤ Microsoft NNTP Service ➤ NNTP Service Manager (HTML).

6. Notice the similarities to the NNTP snap-in for MMC.

7. Close Internet Explorer.

8. Select Start ➤ Programs ➤ Windows NT 4.0 Option Pack ➤ Microsoft Internet Information Server ➤ Microsoft SMTP Service ➤ SMTP Service Manager (HTML).

9. Notice the similarities to the SMTP snap-in for MMC.

10. Close Internet Explorer.

Exam Essentials

Know when to use the MMC for administration. You'll use the MMC for administration whenever possible: when you've got a high bandwidth network and you can participate in normal NT domain security.

Know when to use the HTML service managers for administration. You'll use the HTML service managers when you are remotely administering sites over a TCP/IP network like the Internet or large intranets.

Key Terms and Concepts

HTML service managers: A set of Active Server Pages (ASP) applications organized as a Web site that provide the ability to control the metabase settings that make up a Web site.

Sample Questions

1. You've installed an IIS server at your Internet Service Provider's site so that it can participate on their high-speed Internet backbone directly, rather than being at the slow end of your T1 circuit. You need to determine how you will perform administrative functions like creating new sites remotely. The solution must be secure so

that your IIS server can withstand hacking attempts from the Internet. You can configure your firewall to pass any network traffic you want between your site and the remote server.

Proposed Solution #1: Install the remote server. Enable Windows networking so that you can connect to the server using the MMC. Open the firewall to allow Windows networking protocols to pass.

Proposed Solution #2: Install the remote server. Use the HTML service managers to manage the Web sites and disable the Workstation, RPC, and Server services on the remote IIS server.

Choose the best answer:

A. Neither will work.

B. Both will work, but Solution #1 is preferable.

C. Both will work, but Solution #2 is preferable.

D. Both will work equally well.

Answer: C. This solution prevents a wide range of hacking exploits, and is optimized for low bandwidth connections. Solution #1 will work but opens your IIS server up to a wide range of security holes.

Install and configure Certificate Server.

This objective concerns the installation and configuration of Certificate Server.

Critical Information

Secure Socket Layer (SSL) protects the communications between the Web server and the Web browser for purposes such as commercial transactions (e.g., credit card orders) or for accessing confidential information. Secure Socket Layer does not protect your Internet site from intrusion. Instead, it protects the communications between your Internet site and Web browsers from interception and eavesdropping. When a Web browser connects to a directory on your server that has the Require Secure Channel option enabled, an encrypted link is established between the browser and the server, and sensitive information such as passwords and credit card information can then be transferred back and forth.

When you install a key with a signed certificate into the WWW service, you can then require SSL access to WWW service directories. The Require SSL Channel option on the Directory Security tab (which you cannot get to until you install a key) then becomes available. It is clear by default; you can check this option and require all accesses to the directory to be encrypted.

Web servers like IIS require more processing power, more bandwidth, and more time to send encrypted data than they do to send unencrypted data. You should therefore require SSL only on directories that contain sensitive data or Web pages that receive privileged information such as credit card numbers.

Certificates resolve the uncertainty faced by users of Web browsers visiting your site who have no assurance that you are who you say you are. When an individual visits your Web site, that person *can* assume that you are a legitimate business selling software or any other product over the Web, but you could just as well be an impostor with a bogus Web site, illicitly set up by unscrupulous individuals to capture credit card numbers.

Certificates and certificate authorities assure Web users that your Web site is registered with a responsible organization and is safe to visit. A certificate is a message from that responsible organization (the certificate authority) that identifies your server and resides on your server. Your server can give that message to Web browsers to identify itself.

Microsoft IIS requires a certificate from a certificate authority before you can require SSL on a directory. (The Require SSL option is grayed out in the WWW Service Properties/Directory Properties windows until you install a valid certificate in a key for your Web server.) With

IIS4, you can be your own certificate authority by installing the Certificate Server package in the Windows NT 4 Option Pack. If you act as your own certificate authority, however, visitors to your Web site do not get the benefit of knowing that your Web site credentials have been scrutinized by a respected third party (unless you join your Certificate Server to a Certificate Authority Hierarchy).

Installing Certificate Server is easy. In fact, you installed Certificate Server along with IIS, Index Server, and many other Windows NT Option Pack components earlier in this chapter. Once Certificate Server is installed, it starts automatically and is configured to issue certificates.

There are two things you can do to configure the Certificate Server service after you have installed it: you can change the startup options for the service and you can change the account that Certificate Server uses when processing certificates. If you don't need to process certificates often, then configuring Certificate Server to start up manually may be a good idea; you really shouldn't change the account Certificate Server uses, however, unless you have a good reason to do so.

Creating and installing the certificates issued by Certificate Server is performed using the Key Manager, which is covered in the next chapter.

Necessary Procedures

Since you will rarely actually use Certificate Server once you've created the certificates you need for your site, it's a good idea to use the following procedure to set the service to start manually. You can then start the service whenever you need to issue certificates.

1. Select Start ➤ Settings ➤ Control Panel.

2. Double-click Services.

3. Scroll to the Certificate Authority service and select it.

4. Click Startup.

5. Select Manual.

6. Click OK.

7. Click Stop. Remember to start the certificate service before issuing certificates.

8. Close the Services control panel.

9. Close the Control Panel Window.

Exam Essentials

Understand the purpose of Certificate Server.   Certificate Server allows you to generate your own certificates by digitally signing keys created using the Key Manager.

Key Terms and Concepts

Certificates: Certificates are unforgeable digital signature files that prove to clients that you have been sanctioned to generate keys by a responsible authority.

Keys: Keys are the mathematical ciphers used to encrypt and decrypt secure messages.

Secure Socket Layer (SSL):   SSL encrypts the communication stream between two computers to keep it private while it flows over a public medium like the Internet.

Sample Questions

1. What tool do you use to generate keys?

   A. User Manager

   B. Key Manager

   C. Certificate Server

   D. Microsoft Management Console

   Answer: B. The Certificate Server digitally signs keys created by the Key Manager.

Install and configure Microsoft SMTP Service.

The Simple Mail Transfer Protocol (SMTP) is the Internet standard for transmitting and routing mail on the Internet. It is a server-to-server back-end standard. When you check your mail from a client computer, you are using a different mail protocol called the Post Office Protocol (POP) to retrieve your mail from an SMTP server that has received it and is storing it for you. IIS4 does not come with a POP server, so can only be used to generate mail and to receive mail at a single mail drop. The SMTP service is specifically provided to mail-enable Web sites.

Critical Information

You can install the SMTP service simply by checking the SMTP option under the IIS component when you run the Option Pack setup wizard—in fact, if you've followed the installation procedure presented at the beginning of this chapter, you already have SMTP installed. There can be only one mail server per machine—unlike the Web and FTP services, support for more than one mail service is not provided with the SMTP service in Option Pack for NT Server 4.

Once it is installed, you'll notice an SMTP node in the Microsoft Management Console. All mail configuration is performed through this node or through the HTML SMTP Service Manager, which is similar.

As with the other services, you configure settings by right-clicking the service node and selecting Properties. This brings up a dialog box with the following panes:

- **SMTP Site** controls features that apply to the site in general, such as description, IP address, port, and logging.

- **Operators** allows you to add NTFS security accounts that are allowed to manage the SMTP service.

- **Messages** controls the size of messages and connections.

- **Delivery** allows you to change the undeliverable timings and establish connections to other mail hosts.

- **Directory Security** allows you to establish authentication methods, Secure Socket Layer connection requirements, IP-based address restrictions, and SMTP relay restrictions.

Browse through the various settings and features of the SMTP service.

Sending and receiving messages using the SMTP service is performed a number of different ways. You can write scripts using VBScript or other programming languages that access the programming interface provided to create mail. You can also simply specify the SMTP service as the SMTP server in your mail client and create messages. Or you can copy properly formatted text files into the SMTP Pickup directory, which the SMTP service will automatically scan and deliver.

The following mail folders are used by the SMTP service for the function indicated:

- **Badmail** holds undeliverable mail.

- **Drop** receives all mail messages for the domain.

- **Pickup** processes outgoing mail messages that are copied into the directory.

- **Queue** holds messages awaiting further processing when they can't be delivered immediately.

TIP   Check the online documentation for the SMTP service for more information on its workings.

Necessary Procedures

Use the following procedure to limit the maximum size of an e-mail message and to limit the size of a single session:

1. Start the Microsoft Management Console.

2. Expand the hierarchical view to show the SMTP service.

3. Right-click Default SMTP Site and select Properties.

4. Select the Messages tab.

5. Check the Limit Messages tab.

6. Enter **2048** in the Maximum message size (kilobytes) input box. This limits the size of an individual e-mail message.

7. Enter **8192** in the Maximum session size (kilobytes) input box. This limits the duration of a single transmission session to the size indicated. More sessions will be created as necessary to transmit all queued mail.

8. Click OK.

Exam Essentials

The SMTP service is not a major part of the exam, but you should be familiar with how to change various SMTP service settings.

Know how to modify the SMTP undeliverable timings.   Modify SMTP undeliverable timings by right-clicking the SMTP service node, selecting Properties, clicking the Delivery tab, and changing the value for the Maximum Number of Retries and the Retry Interval.

Know how to modify SMTP message size limits.   Modify SMTP message size limits by right-clicking the SMTP service node, selecting Properties, clicking the Messages tab, and changing the value for the Maximum Message Size.

Know how to enable SMTP service transaction logs. Enable SMTP service transaction logs by right-clicking the SMTP service node, selecting Properties, clicking the SMTP Site tab, and checking the Enable Logging option.

Key Terms and Concepts

Message: A text message with an addressed recipient in the form user@server.domain. SMTP forwards messages to the server specified after the @ symbol. The message server is then responsible for delivery to the user specified before the @ symbol.

Relay: A mail host that simply forwards mail—it is neither the originating server nor the final recipient.

Sample Questions

1. Choose the sequence that enables SMTP service transaction logs to create a new log every month using the Microsoft IIS Log File Format:

   A. Select the Default SMTP Site, select Action ➤ Properties, check Enable Logging, click OK.

   B. Select the local host, select Action ➤ Properties, select SMTP Service in the Master Properties pick box, check Enable Logging, select Microsoft IIS Log File Format, click OK.

   C. Select the default SMTP Site, select Action ➤ Properties, select SMTP Service in the Master Properties pick box, check Enable Logging, select Microsoft IIS Log File Format, click Properties, select Monthly, click OK, click OK.

   D. Select the local host, select Action ➤ Properties, select SMTP Service in the Master Properties pick box, check Enable Logging, select Microsoft IIS Log File Format, click OK.

   Answer: C. Other options either don't work or do not complete the requirement.

Install and configure Microsoft NNTP Service.

This objective deals with the Net News Transfer Protocol (also referred to as UseNet News or simply News), which replicates messages from news clients around the network or Internet between all participating news servers. NNTP is often used for support forums or community-based special interest sites because of its convenient, timely, and public dispersion of information between users.

Critical Information

Installing the NNTP protocol is done as part of the regular Option Pack installation and is covered under the first objective in this chapter. As with all other services, configuration is performed through the Microsoft Management Console. There is also an HTML-based NNTP Service Manager you can use for remote administration, but knowledge of its use is not required for testing purposes.

Unlike Web and FTP services, you can only have one NNTP site per server. This site is called the default NNTP site, and it is automatically created when you install the NNTP service.

Newsgroups, or topics of discussion, are managed as directories from the NNTP root by the NNTP service. To create a new topic, you simply create a new directory in the C:\Inetpub\nntpfile\root directory (or other root if you've changed the default). When users create groups on your news server, directories to contain their messages are automatically created by the service.

You manage the NNTP service from the Microsoft Management Console by right-clicking on the default NNTP site and selecting an option from the menu presented.

NNTP supports virtual directories exactly the same way that the Web and FTP services do, except that NNTPs contain newsgroups rather than Web or FTP files. You can set NNTP virtual directories to a path on the local machine or to another machine, and you can control whether the group is read-only or writable (allows posting). You can restrict newsgroup visibility so that users without permission to see content can't see the newsgroup listed, and you can indicate whether or not Index Server should index the content of that newsgroup.

You can also set expiration policies for the entire site as well as for individual newsgroups. Expiration policies determine how long messages are kept before being automatically deleted. You can set messages to expire based on their date and their size.

You can enable logging for NTTP the same way you can enable logging for the FTP and Web services.

Necessary Procedures

Use the following procedure to create an NNTP virtual directory:

1. Start the MMC.

2. Right-click the Default NNTP Site and select New ➤ Virtual Directory.

3. Enter **test** in the newsgroup name input box.

4. Enter **c:\temp** in the path input box.

5. Expand the Default NNTP Site.

6. Select the Directories node.

7. Double-click the test directory.

8. Check Index news content.

9. Click OK.

10. Right-click the test directory and select Delete.

11. Click Yes.

12. Close the MMC.

Exam Essentials

Know the purpose of the NNTP service. NNTP serves topical public messages and allows users to post new messages or replies to current messages. NNTP is typically used for technical support bulletin boards or special interest community discussions.

Know how to create NNTP virtual directories. Create NNTP virtual directories by right-clicking on the default NNTP site and selecting New ➤ Virtual Directory.

Understand the proper way to use Index Server with the NNTP service. Index Server will automatically search NNTP sites if you enable the Index News Content checkbox in the Home Directory section of the default site or virtual directories.

Know how to enable NNTP service logging. Enable NNTP service logging by checking the Enable Logging checkbox on the News Site tab of the default NNTP site Properties dialog box and selecting the style of logging you want to use.

Key Terms and Concepts

Net News Transfer Protocol (NNTP): A protocol for transferring message-based entries of a hierarchical database between servers called news servers.

Newsgroup: A related set of messages all based on the same topic.

Sample Questions

1. Create a virtual directory for the NNTP service to store the test.results newsgroup in the g:\results directory. Choose the correct sequence:

    A. Right-click the NNTP site, select New ➤ Virtual Directory, enter **test.results** in the Newsgroup Name, click Next, enter **g:\results**, click Finish.

    B. Right-click the NNTP site, select Properties, select the Directories tab, click New, enter **test.results** in the Newsgroup Name, click Next, enter **g:\results**, click Finish.

    C. Right-click the NNTP site, select Properties, select Groups, click Create New Newsgroup, enter **test.results** in the Newsgroup Name, click OK.

    D. Right-click the NNTP site, select Properties, select Groups, click Create New Newsgroup, enter **test.results** in the Newsgroup Name, enter **g:\results** in the path input box, click OK.

Answer: A. C creates a newsgroup in the root directory, not in a virtual directory, and the other options won't work.

2. Enable NNTP Service logging using W3C Extended Log File Format. Choose the correct sequence:

    A. Right-click Default NNTP site, select Properties, check Enable Logging, click OK.

    B. Right-click your Internet Server, select Properties, click Edit, check Enable Logging, click OK, click OK.

    C. Right-click your Internet Server, select Properties, click Edit, check Enable Logging, select W3C Extended Log File Format, click OK, click OK.

    D. Right-click Default NNTP site, select Properties, check Enable Logging, select W3C Extended Log File Format, click OK.

Answer: D. A selects Microsoft logging format, and B and C modify Web site logging, not NNTP logging.

Customize the installation of Microsoft Site Server Express Content Analyzer.

This objective is one of several covering Site Server Express, a "lite" version of the commercial Site Server product that is used to manage and maintain Web sites. Site Server Express comprises these components:

- Content Analyzer, which analyzes Web pages to map out the structure of a Web site

- Report Writer, which digests information from IIS logs to create meaningful, concise reports

- Usage Import, which is used to import log information for Report Writer from IIS

This objective covers the first component, Content Analyzer.

Critical Information

Microsoft's Site Server Express helps you keep track of your Web pages, informing you of how many pages you are hosting, what the average number of links per page are, how much space is being taken up by images, sound, or video, and how often those pages are being accessed.

The Content Analyzer is the tool you use to manage what is stored in the directories of your Web site (unlike the Microsoft Management Console, which concerns itself primarily with the directories themselves and how the browser connects to them).

If you use a Web browser other than Internet Explorer, if you need to connect to your Web site through a proxy server, or if you need to be able to analyze Web pages protected by passwords, then you will have to specially configure Content Analyzer.

You configure Content Analyzer through the Program Options window, which you get to from the Program Options... item in the View menu. The Program Options window has five tabs:

- **General** allows you to specify which browser to use with Content Analyzer and how to connect to the Web site being analyzed.

- **Helpers** allows you to configure helper applications to be launched when you view or edit any defined object type.

- **Proxy** allows you to configure Content Analyzer to work through a proxy server.

- **Cyberbolic** allows you to change how the cyberbolic view of a Web site behaves.

- **Passwords** allows you to configure any passwords that the Content Analyzer may need to access protected directories on Web sites.

NOTE Content Analyzer uses Basic Authentication to connect to password-protected resources, so if you want Content Analyzer to map those portions of your Web site you will have to make sure that Basic Authentication is enabled.

Once you've installed and configured Content Analyzer, you can create a Web map to see and browse a graphical view of your Web site. This allows you to quickly identify and fix broken links and other Web site problems. You can create Web maps from two sources:

- Files of sites stored on your network

- URLs of active Internet sites

Content Analyzer can automatically explore your Web site no matter what the source and find the pages it's linked to. You can set constraints to limit how many pages it will add to your site or whether it will explore links to other sites. Figure 2.3 shows the Content Analyzer displaying a cyberbolic view of a Web site.

FIGURE 2.3: A cyberbolic Web map

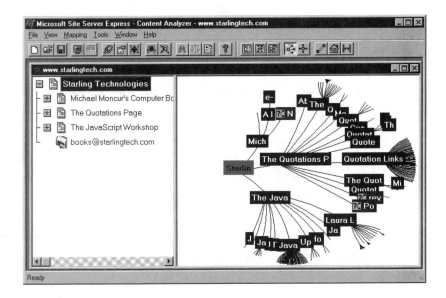

Necessary Procedures

Use the following procedure to configure Content Analyzer to work through a proxy server if you have one.

1. Select Start ➤ Programs ➤ Windows NT 4.0 Option Pack ➤ Microsoft Site Server Express 2.0 ➤ Content Analyzer.

2. Click Open Web Map.

3. Double-click Sample.wmp.

4. Select View ➤ Program Options.

5. Select the Proxy tab.

6. Select Custom Proxy Configuration.

7. Enter the IP address of your Proxy Server (e.g.: **10.1.1.1**).

8. Enter the port number for the HTTP Proxy Service on that server (e.g.: **8080.**)

9. Click OK.

10. Close the Content Analyzer.

Exam Essentials

Understand the purpose of Content Analyzer and when you would use it. Content Analyzer is used primarily to maintain Web site content like HTML pages. Content Analyzer is capable of analyzing a site to quickly find errors.

Key Terms and Concepts

Cyberbolic: A graphical view of Web page relationships that changes to display the relationships from the currently selected page.

Sample Questions

1. You've noticed a number of broken links while browsing your company's Web site. What tool will help you fix these broken links the fastest? (Choose all that apply.)

    A. Report Writer

    B. Content Analyzer

    C. Usage Import

    D. Microsoft Management Console

    Answer: B. Content Analyzer is used to analyze Web site content.

Customize the installation of Microsoft Site Server Express Usage Import and Report Writer.

This objective covers two of the three components of Site Server Express:

- Report Writer, which digests information from IIS logs to create meaningful, concise reports

- Usage Import, which is used to import log information for Report Writer from IIS

Critical Information

Site Server Express creates a summary report for you automatically (unless you tell it not to) and displays it in your Web browser when you create an initial Web map. Microsoft Site Server (the commercial version, which is not included with Internet Information Server 4) has additional reports that can tell you more about your Web site. The summary report is divided into three parts:

- **Object Statistics**   This part lists the number and size of the objects stored in your Web site, broken down by their type (such as HTML pages, Java classes, image files, and so on).

- **Status Summary**   This part describes the links in your Web site, separated into on-site and off-site links, and shows the number of good links, bad links, missing links, and unverified links.

- **Map Statistics**   This part gives you such miscellaneous information as when the map was made, how "deep" it got, and the average number of links on a page in the Web site.

Report Writer is another major component of Site Server Express.

The logs created by IIS are a gold mine of information on how your server is used. Logs are useful for figuring out how well your server performs over time and what parts of your Web site(s) are the most popular and therefore are consuming the most bandwidth on your server.

Unfortunately, these logs create an enormous amount of information. You can log to an ODBC data source like a Microsoft Access database or an SQL Server, query the data, and then create reports to view any statistics you want, but that process takes a lot of setup effort. Report Writer can perform much of this work for you.

Report Writer is the part of Site Server Express that takes the log data stored by IIS and helps you understand how your site is being accessed. With Report Writer (and Usage Import) you can easily separate out important information from the voluminous amount of data a busy Web site can generate. You can track such data as the most frequently accessed pages, the most common errors, the times of greatest site access, and even where most of your accesses come from. To use Report Writer, you must have IIS4 logging configured to log the information you want. Report Writer can import from any of the logging formats.

The Usage Import tool imports formatted log files into the Jet database format used by Report Writer (the same format used by Microsoft Access). Usage Import is capable of performing reverse DNS lookups to resolve the IP addresses stored in log files to the DNS names of the computers that access your site, Whois queries to determine which organization owns the computer in question, and title lookup, which opens the HTML page referenced in the log entry to extract the page's title. These operations consume an enormous amount of network bandwidth and time (taking several seconds per entry), so you should only do them when you've got plenty of time and bandwidth to spare. You can automate the Usage Import tool using the Scheduler service. Note that automated Usage Imports that use any of the above resolution tools will take a lot of time, so they should only be scheduled for periods of network inactivity. Figure 2.4 shows the Usage Import tool.

FIGURE 2.4: The Usage Import tool

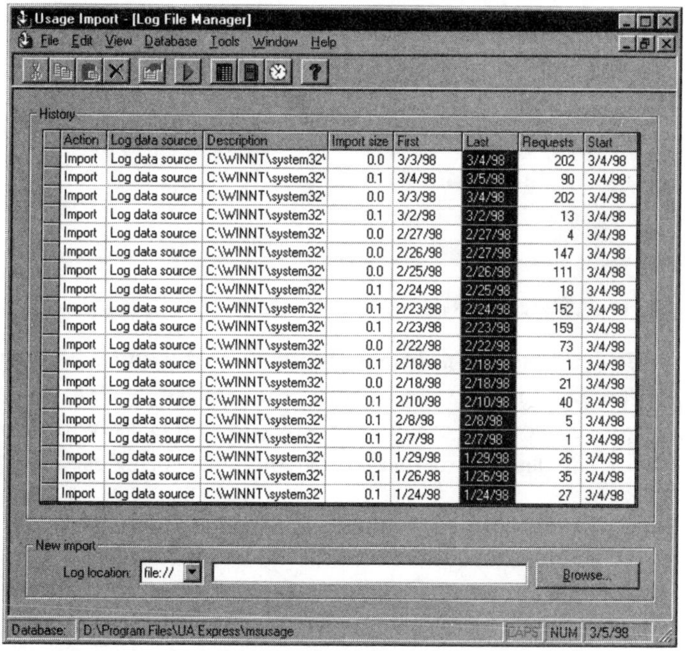

Necessary Procedures

1. Select Start ➤ Programs ➤ Windows NT 4.0 Option Pack ➤ Microsoft Site Server Express 2.0 ➤ Report Writer.

2. Click OK.

3. Double-click Summary Reports.

4. Double-click Executive Report.

5. Click Finish.

6. Select File ➤ Create Report Document.

7. Enter **c:\report.htm** in the file name input box.

8. When the report is finished, Internet Explorer will launch automatically. Browse the report using Internet Explorer.

9. Close Internet Explorer.

10. Click Close in the Report Writer dialog box.

11. Close the Report Writer.

Exam Essentials

Understand the purpose of Report Writer and when you would use it. Report Writer creates easily understandable, concise reports from the volumes of raw data provided by IIS logs. With Report Writer, you can determine exactly how your site is being used and by whom.

Understand the purpose of Usage Import and its requirements. Usage Import translates IIS logs into Microsoft Jet databases that can be parsed by Report Writer. It also translates IP addresses into DNS names, performs Whois lookups to return organizational information, and performs title lookups on HTML pages. These operations are very lengthy and bandwidth-consuming, so they should be scheduled to run during periods of network inactivity.

Key Terms and Concepts

Reporting: The process of condensing massive amounts of data into concise informative facts.

Sample Questions

1. You want to tune the bandwidth settings of your various Web sites to keep some from overwhelming other, more important sites that sustain lower usage. What tool will help you determine how Internet browsers are using the several Web sites on your server? (Choose all that apply.)

   A. Report Writer

   B. Content Analyzer

   C. Usage Import

   D. Microsoft Management Console

   Answer: A, C, and **D.** Report Writer and Usage Import work together to create reports from IIS service logs, which must be configured using the Microsoft Management Console.

CHAPTER

3

Configuring and
Managing Resource Access

Microsoft Exam Objectives Covered in This Chapter:

▶ **Create and share directories with appropriate permissions.**
Tasks include: *(pages 99 – 110)*
- Setting directory-level permissions
- Setting file-level permissions

▶ **Create and share local and remote virtual directories with appropriate permissions. Tasks include:** *(pages 110 – 116)*
- Creating a virtual directory and assigning an alias
- Setting directory-level permissions
- Setting file-level permissions

▶ **Create and share virtual servers with appropriate permissions.**
Tasks include: *(pages 117 – 118)*
- Assigning IP addresses

▶ **Write scripts to manage the FTP service or the WWW service.**
(pages 119 – 122)

▶ **Manage a Web site by using Content Analyzer. Tasks include:** *(pages 122 – 131)*
- Creating, customizing, and navigating WebMaps
- Examining a Web site by using the various reports provided by Content Analyzer
- Tracking links by using a WebMap

▶ **Configure Microsoft SMTP Service to host message traffic.**
(pages 132 – 141)

▶ **Configure Microsoft NNTP Service to host a newsgroup.**
(pages 141 – 146)

▶ **Configure Certificate Server to issue certificates.**
(pages 146 – 152)

▶ **Configure Index Server to index a Web site.** *(pages 152 – 157)*

▶ **Manage MIME types.** *(pages 157 – 159)*

▶ **Manage the FTP service.** *(pages 160 – 161)*

▶ **Manage the WWW service.** *(pages 161 – 163)*

Create and share directories with appropriate permissions. Tasks include:

- Setting directory-level permissions
- Setting file-level permissions

This objective concerns those things you need to understand about NT file system permissions and Windows networking to properly control access and to support using virtual directories.

SEE ALSO   Refer to Mark Minasi's excellent book *Mastering Windows NT Server 4* (Sybex, 1997) for more information about NT file system permissions.

Critical Information

Users identify themselves to Windows NT by providing logon credentials that the system compares to an access control list (ACL) containing individual permission entries maintained for each object the user attempts to access. Permissions are applied to just about every operating system object, but the two most important objects are network shares and file system objects like files and directories.

Your access token is created when you log on. It contains your user identity and the identity of all groups you belong to. The system compares the access token to the ACL of each secured resource (such as a share, file, or directory) you attempt to access. These resources contain ACLs that list each security ID from the user accounts and groups permitted to use the resource. If any of the identifiers in your access token match identifiers in a resource's ACL, you are allowed access as specified by that entry.

Share Permissions

Share permissions control access to shared resources. Directories that have been shared have four levels of permissions that can be assigned to various users and groups. Table 3.1 shows the different share-level permissions that can be assigned and their effects. Keep in mind that the default share permissions assignment is Full Control to the group Everyone—this is almost never correct. You should usually remove this permission and apply permissions individually for the users and groups who actually need access to this resource.

T A B L E 3.1: Share Permissions Properties

Permission	Effect
No Access	Prevents access to the shared directory.
Read	Allows viewing of contained files and directories, loading of files, and the execution of software.
Change	Allows all read permissions plus creating, deleting, and changing contained directories and files.
Full Control	Allows all change permissions plus changing file system permissions and taking ownership.

Windows NT does not use share permissions to control access to the Internet host itself. Internet users are logged on locally to the Internet host, so share permissions for that machine usually do not affect them. However, that host may be logged on to other machines and serving data stored in those other machines through the virtual directory mechanism. In that case, share permissions do affect which shares can be accessed. Although share permissions will affect the ability to access those resources, you will normally use file system permissions, rather than share permissions, to secure data on Internet hosts.

Share permissions work regardless of the file system security measures you may have implemented with either the FAT or NT file system, so you can use them on both NTFS and FAT shared volumes. If you have directory permissions set up on an NTFS volume, users will be restricted by both sets of permissions.

TIP   Windows NT selects the most restrictive permission when combining share permissions and file system permissions.

NT File System Permissions

File system permissions complement the basic share-level permissions. The FAT file system does not have a set of file and directory attributes rich enough to implement security on a file or directory basis, so file system permissions are not available for FAT-formatted volumes. The server service in the Windows NT operating system implements share permissions to secure access to file systems that did not implement security.

WARNING   File system permissions are available only for NTFS (New Technology File System) volumes, not for FAT volumes. You cannot properly secure your Web site without using file system permissions. Your Internet site files and system integrity could be compromised unless you use the NT file system and properly configure security for all the Internet publication directories. Only Windows NT computers can read NTFS volumes.

NTFS implements security control over the sharing of information with file system permissions, which are assigned to individual files and directories using file system attribute bits that are stored in the directory tables of the file system. Consequently, file system permissions work even on stand-alone computers. For instance, if Jane creates a directory in an NTFS volume and assigns permissions for only herself, then no one else can access that directory (except administrators who can always take ownership of the directory) even when logged on to the same machine.

> **NOTE** Since Web users are logged on locally to the Web server, normally only NT file system permissions are effective for security.

File system permissions can also be used to restrict which files are available to a user. Therefore, even though share permissions may allow access to a directory, file system permissions can still restrict it. When both NT file system permissions and share permissions are applied, the more restrictive permissions will take precedence. Table 3.2 shows the effect of NTFS directory permissions.

T A B L E 3.2: Directory Permissions

Permission	Effect
No Access	Prevents any access to the directory and its files.
List	View filenames; browse directories. Does not allow access to files unless overridden by other file or directory permissions.
Read	Open files and execute applications.
Add	Add files and subdirectories without Read access.
Change	Incorporates Add and Read permissions and adds the ability to delete files and directories.
Full Control	Allows Change and Take Ownership permissions and authority to assign permissions.

Conflicting Permissions

With the myriad shares, groups, files, and directories that can be created in a network environment, some resource permission conflicts are bound to occur. When a user is a member of many groups, some of those groups may specifically allow access to a resource while other group memberships deny it. Also, cumulative permissions may occur. For example, a user may have Read access to a directory because he's a domain user and also have Full Control because he's a member of the Engineers group. Windows NT determines access privileges in the following manner:

- A specific denial (the No Access permission) always overrides specific access to a resource.

- When resolving conflicts between share permissions and file permissions, Windows NT chooses the most restrictive. For instance, if the share permission allows full control but the file permissions allow read-only, the file is read-only.

- When a user is a member of multiple groups, the user always has the combined permissions of all group memberships and any individual permissions assigned to the user account.

NTFS defines access permissions based on file system operations. Because useful permissions usually require more than one file system operation, the file system permissions you can assign are actually combinations of permitted file system operations. Table 3.3 shows the file system operations that are allowed, and Table 3.4 shows the combinations that are formed to create actual permissions. The question marks in the Special Access row of Table 3.4 signify that special access provides a way to create your own combinations of file system operation permissions to create complex special accesses.

T A B L E 3.3: File System Operations

Operation	Description
R	Read or display data, attributes, owner, and permissions.
X	Run or execute the file or files in the directory.
W	Write to the file or directory or change the attributes.
D	Delete the file or directory.
P	Change permissions.
O	Take ownership.

T A B L E 3.4: Combined Access Permissions

Permission	R	X	W	D	P	O
No Access						
List (Directory only)	X					
Read	X	X				
Add (Directory only)		X	X			
Add & Read (Directory Only)	X	X	X			
Change	X	X	X	X		
Full Control	X	X	X	X	X	X
Special File (or Directory) Access	?	?	?	?	?	?

Each access permission performs a specific set of operations on the file or directory, which can allow or disallow any combination of tasks.

Copying and Moving Files with Permissions

When you copy a file (or a directory) from one directory on an NTFS or FAT partition to another directory on the same or a different partition, the file inherits the share and file permissions and owner of the receiving directory.

Moving a file or directory from one directory to another on the same partition does not change the permissions and owner of that file or directory. However, if you move files across partitions, the permissions change to that of the new directory.

The difference between copying and moving files is that when you copy a file, the original file still resides in its original location. You are essentially creating a new file in the new location that contains the same data as the old file. The new file (the copy) will have the receiving directory's new-file permissions.

When a directory is copied, it receives the directory and default new-file permissions of its new parent directory. As the new files are created within the new directory, they receive the new-file permissions of this directory.

Moving a file or directory within the same partition, instead of copying it, merely changes pointers in the directory structure on the existing FAT or NTFS partition. The file or directory disappears from the old location and appears in the new location but does not physically move on the hard disk. The file and share permissions and ownership of the file or directory remain the same. A file moved between partitions is treated the same as a file being copied because that is actually what happens.

WARNING   Some programs perform a move command by actually copying the file or directory to the new location and then deleting it from the old location. In this case the file obtains new permissions from the receiving directory, just as it would in a regular copy operation. This effect is sometimes called the *container effect.*

Necessary Procedures

The following procedures walk you through the information presented in this section.

Setting Share-Level Permissions

1. Double-click My Computer.

2. Double-click the C: drive in the My Computer window.

3. Right-click a white area (an area where there are no icons or files).

4. Select New Folder in the pop-up menu that appears.

5. Type **Test Share** as the name of the folder. You must do so immediately or the focus will change. If the focus changes and you can't rename the file, right-click the folder and select the rename option.

6. Right-click your newly created Test Share folder.

7. Select Sharing.

8. Select Shared As:. The name of the folder will automatically appear as the share name. You can change the share name if you wish. This is the name that users will see when they view the folder through browsing features such as Network Neighborhood.

9. Click Permissions.

10. Click Remove to remove the Everyone: Full Control permission.

11. Click Add.

12. Select Domain Users.

13. Select Read in the Type of Access list box.

14. Click OK.

15. Click OK.

16. Click OK.

17. Click Yes to acknowledge the warning about MS-DOS clients.

Setting Directory-Level Permissions

1. Open the My Computer icon on your desktop.

2. Open the (C:) icon (or the icon for the NTFS partition in your computer) in the My Computer window.

3. Right-click on an empty area of the window and select New ➤ Folder. Type **test** to name the folder and hit Enter. Make sure the folder remains selected.

4. Select File ➤ Properties.

5. Select the Security tab.

6. Click the Permissions button.

7. Select the Everyone group in the Directory Permissions window and then click Remove.

8. Click Add.

9. Click the Show Users button. Select IUSR_*computername*. Click Add. Select Read in the Type of Access pick list. Click OK.

10. Click Add. Select Administrators. Click Add. Select Full Control in the Type of Access pick list. Click OK.

11. Click OK in the permissions window and then click OK in the Directory permissions window. Click OK to close the Properties window.

Setting File-Level Permissions

1. Double-click the test folder you created in the previous exercise.

2. Right-click on a blank area in the test folder window and select New ➤ Text Document. Hit Enter.

3. Right-click on the New Text Document icon and select Properties.

4. Click the Security tab. Click the Permissions button.

5. Notice that the ACL for the file matches the ACL of the containing directory.

6. Select the IUSR_*computername* access control entry and click Remove.

7. Click Add. Select Users. Select Change in the Type of Access pick list. Click OK.

8. Click OK.

9. Click OK.

Exam Essentials

The following information is crucial to the exam:

Understand the logon authentication method.   Since every user of a Windows NT System like a file or Web server must be logged in, each person's authenticated identity in the form of a security identifier can be attached to every request they make of the system. This allows Windows NT to determine, based on the identity of a user, whether or not access should be granted to a particular resource.

Understand file system permissions. Every file system object (files and directories) contains a list of the users and groups of users that are allowed to access the object and in what manner. When an authenticated user attempts to access that resource, its permissions are checked to determine what manner of access, if any, is allowed to that user.

Know how to change NT file system permissions. Changing NT file system permissions can be performed by right-clicking on a file system object, selecting Properties, clicking the Permissions tab, and adding identity/permission pairs called access control entries (ACEs) to the ACL for the object.

Key Terms and Concepts

Access Control Entry (ACE): A single account (group or user) associated with a permission such as Read, Write, Change, or No Access.

Access Control List (ACL): A list of ACEs attached to an object. Every object has an ACL.

Directory: A container for files and other directories in hierarchical namespace. Directories provide convenient objects to group and manage related files.

File: Data stored on a file system that is located by a filename and associated with other parameters such as access permissions.

Permissions: A list of accounts and corresponding types of access attached to an object (e.g., shares, files, printers), which is used to determine the functions those accounts are allowed to perform on the object.

Sample Questions

1. You've implemented a Web site on your file server and intend to use NT file system security to secure the site. When you right-click the directory that you intend to secure and select Properties, you

notice that there's no Security tab so you can't set file system security. What's wrong?

A. The volume is formatted with the FAT file system.

B. You haven't turned on file auditing.

C. You haven't enabled file system security in the Internet Service Manager.

D. You aren't logged in as the administrator so you can't change security permissions.

Answer: A. FAT volumes have no security options.

2. Your Web site is secured using the following permissions:

IUSR_*computername*	Read
Everyone	No Access
Domain Users	Change

Additionally, you've set IIS access permissions to Read, and you've disabled anonymous access through the Directory Security tab. Users complain that they cannot access the Web site through their browsers. How can you correct the problem?

A. Enable anonymous access using the Microsoft Management Console.

B. Set the IUSR_*computername* permission to Change using the desktop Explorer.

C. Delete the Everyone ACE using the desktop Explorer.

D. Set the Domain Users permission to Read.

Answer: C. In this case, the specific No Access permission for Everyone overrides all other access permissions.

3. Increased reliance on your corporate intranet has caused the site to grow larger than originally anticipated. You install another hard disk in your Web server, format it with the NT file system, and copy your site files to the new volume. You then configure the IIS services to point to the new locations using the virtual directory

feature, making sure that your directory access settings are exactly the same as before. Suddenly, all users have access to the formerly secured financial directories. Why did this happen?

A. You've used the wrong file system on the new hard disk drive.

B. You've improperly configured IIS directory access security for the virtual directories in the Microsoft Management Console.

C. The new site is allowing anonymous access.

D. NTFS permissions were reset when you copied the files between volumes.

Answer: D. Copying files between volumes causes those files to receive the NTFS permissions of the parent directory on the new volume.

Create and share local and remote virtual directories with appropriate permissions. Tasks include:

- Creating a virtual directory and assigning an alias
- Setting directory-level permissions
- Setting file-level permissions

This objective concerns the creation and management of virtual directories. Virtual directories allow you to reference directories located on other volumes or machines as subdirectories in your Web site directory by an alias that you assign.

Virtual directories do not actually exist inside your root directory, but they appear to Web browsers as if they do. You can think of them as shortcuts to other locations on your server or other servers.

Critical Information

Virtual directories allow you to share Internet data that exists in directories other than your Web, NNTP, or FTP root directories by creating a "virtual" subdirectory alias that points to the physical location of the data. That data can reside anywhere on your network that is accessible to your Web server. Virtual directories are also useful for redirecting browsers to other directories. For instance, say one of your customers has moved their Web site off of your server. Rather than deleting their files and leaving Web browsers in the dark, you can simply change their virtual directory to redirect browsers to the URL of the new site.

The following can be used to identify the data source for virtual directories:

- a directory located on a local drive (or mapped network drive) referenced by directory path

- a share located anywhere on your network referenced by UNC path

- a redirection to another HTTP server referenced by URL

Virtual directories also give you the ability to control IIS service security inside your Web site. For instance, if you have a directory to which you would like to allow uploads, you can create a virtual directory inside your FTP site that allows writing. The rest of your FTP site remains protected by the IIS service security setting to allow only reading. You can control the following security settings separately for each virtual directory:

- Read

- Write

- Log Access

- Directory Browsing Allowed

- Index This Directory

- FrontPage Web administrable

In addition to those security settings, you can also control the following application settings:

- Application name and configuration

- Run in Separate Memory Space

- None (Permissions)

- Script (Permissions)

- Execute (Permissions)

NOTE   Virtual directories do not appear in HTTP directory listings or FTP directories. To access a virtual directory from an index list, the browser must know the name and enter it in the address line. You can work around this problem by creating an empty actual directory with the same name as the virtual directory alias.

Virtual Directories on Foreign Domains/ Workgroups (map drive or use UNC)

There are two ways to specify that data for a virtual directory should come from a foreign computer:

- **Map a drive,** and then specify a normal path. This option requires that you specify a drive using the Map Network Drive setting, and then enter the path to the data as you would for any other volume. Although this solution may seem more natural to those used to working with drive letters, it can potentially cause problems. The drive may for some reason become unmapped, and then your Web site would no longer work. Also, fewer than 26 drive letters are available for mapping, so large Web sites that span many computers would not have enough drive letters to map them all.

- **Use the UNC path.** This option does not require any prior setup in the desktop Explorer, and works no matter what your drive letter mappings are. For these reasons, specifying the UNC path is the preferred method of identifying remote computers.

Necessary Procedures

The following procedures assume you have started the Microsoft Management Console and have the IIS snap-in expanded to show individual Web sites.

Creating a Virtual Directory and Assigning an Alias

Use the following procedure to create a virtual directory for a Web site. FTP and NNTP virtual directories are created the same way.

1. Right-click on the test Web site you created in the previous chapter.

2. Select New ➤ Virtual Directory.

3. Enter **Admin** in the Alias input box and click Next.

4. Click Browse.

5. Browse to `c:\winnt\system32\inetsrv\iisadmin` and click OK. Replace drive letters and pathnames to match your system directory. Click Next.

6. Click Finish.

You have now created a virtual directory that redirects any access to your site's \admin subdirectory to the administration Web site on your server.

Setting Directory-Level Permissions

Setting the IIS service security for a virtual directory is easily accomplished through the Properties panel of the virtual directory. Use the following procedure to change the virtual directory security settings:

1. Expand the test Web site to show the Admin virtual directory you created in the previous procedure.

2. Right-click on the Admin virtual directory and select Properties.

3. Click the Virtual Directory Properties pane.

4. Check Directory browsing allowed.

5. Check Write access.

6. Click OK.

These settings were used to show the process of changing the IIS service security settings for virtual directories, not to indicate how a production server should be configured. Using the steps above as a guide, go back through and disallow Directory browsing and Write access.

Setting File-Level Permissions

Setting NTFS permissions for documents inside virtual directories is no different than setting permissions for any file system object anywhere. Use the desktop Explorer to browse to the location where the files or directories are stored, right-click on their icon, select Properties, click Permissions, and change their access control list. The exercises in the previous section will walk you through this process if you need a refresher.

Exam Essentials

Understand the concept of virtual directories. Virtual directories allow data stored in other locations to appear to Web browsers as subdirectories of your Web site. Virtual directories can also be used to redirect browsers to other Web sites, and to change IIS security settings for specific directories inside your site.

Use NT file system permissions to control access to virtual directories. You use NT file system permissions to finely control access to the data stored in virtual directories in the same manner that you would use them to control access to anything on your server.

Key Terms and Concepts

Alias: The name used to refer to a virtual directory. The alias shows up as a subdirectory inside the Web site.

Universal Naming Convention (UNC):   A standardized method for referring to data located on foreign servers, taking the form *\\server\share\directorypath\data*, where *server* is the Windows name of the server, *share* is the share name of the directory that provides the data, *directorypath* is the path inside the share to the specific location being referenced, and *data* is the filename of the file referred to.

Virtual directory: A method for linking data not contained in the directory structure of a Web site to that Web site. The data may be contained on the same volume in another location, on another volume, on another server, or in another Web site.

Sample Questions

1. You want to be able to manage a Web site remotely using your Web browser. You don't want to have to remember the port number that the Administration Web site is using. What should you do?

    A. Create a virtual directory called `iisadmin` in the Web site and point it to the `inetpub\scripts` directory.

    B. Create a virtual directory called `iisadmin` in the Web site and point it to the `inetsrv\iisadmin` subdirectory of your Windows NT System32 directory.

    C. Disable Windows NT Challenge/Response for your network and enable Secure Socket Layer communications for your Web site.

    D. You cannot remotely administer the IIS service.

    Answer: B. You can create a virtual directory in the Web site that points to the `iisadmin` directory. You can then simply type the URL of your Web site followed by `/iisadmin` to administer the Web site.

2. How do you redirect a Web browser that requests a Web site that has moved to another computer on the Internet (not a part of your domain)?

   A. Set the Local Path of the Web site to the UNC path of the new host computer (e.g., *IP address\share name*). Enter a valid username and password for the share.

   B. Change the default document to a document that informs the user that that site no longer exists.

   C. Click the button for A share located on another computer and then set the Network Directory of the Web site to the UNC path of the new host computer (e.g., *IP address\share name*). Enter a valid username and password for the share.

   D. Click the button for A redirection to a URL and enter the new URL to the home site in the Redirect to: field.

   Answer: D. With a redirection IIS simply tells the Web browser where to look for the files, rather than retrieving the files and sending them to the browser.

3. How do you satisfy a Web browser that requests from a Web site files that are now stored on a network share of another computer in your LAN?

   A. Set the Local Path of the Web site to the UNC path of the new host computer (e.g., *computer name\share name*). Enter a valid username and password for the share.

   B. Change the default document to a document that informs the user that that site no longer exists.

   C. Click the button for A share located on another computer and then set the Network Directory of the Web site to the UNC path of the new host computer (e.g., *computer name\share name*). Enter a valid username and password for the share.

   D. Click the button for A redirection to a URL and enter the new URL to the home site in the Redirect to: field.

   Answer: C. When the files have moved to another computer on your LAN but the IIS computer is still serving those Web files to Web browsers, you can configure the Web site to go to that network share to retrieve the files.

Create and share virtual servers with appropriate permissions. Tasks include:

▪ Assigning IP addresses

The information for this objective is exactly the same as the information covered in Chapter 2 under "Create WWW site" in the section "Configure IIS to support the WWW service." That chapter covers the use of host headers and the assignment of IP addresses to Web sites.

Critical Information

Refer to "Configure IIS to support the WWW service" in Chapter 2 for information about the management of the WWW service.

Necessary Procedures

Refer to "Configure IIS to support the WWW service" in Chapter 2 for WWW management procedures.

Exam Essentials

Refer to "Configure IIS to support the WWW service" in Chapter 2 for exam essentials relating to virtual servers.

Key Terms & Concepts

Virtual server: Another term for a Web or FTP site on an IIS4 machine.

Web site: A group of interrelated Web pages with a unified purpose, a similar stylistic theme, and a distinct method of address (either by unique IP address, port, or host header).

Sample Questions

1. Select the correct sequence of actions to create a virtual Web site called Human Resources in the D:\HR directory from the MMC with the distinct IP address of 10.1.1.7 (assuming this address has already been added to the TCP/IP protocol on your machine). (Choose all correct answers.)

   A. Right-click the server and select New ➤ Web Site. Type **Human Resources** and press Enter. Select 10.1.1.7 in the Select IP Address list box. Click Next. Click Next. Click Finish.

   B. Right-click the default Web site and select New ➤ Site. Type **Human Resources** and press Enter. Select 10.1.1.7 in the Select IP Address list box. Click Next. Type **D:\HR** and press Enter. Click Finish.

   C. Right-click the server and select New ➤ Web Site. Type **Human Resources** and press Enter. Select 10.1.1.7 in the Select IP Address list box. Click Next. Type **D:\HR** and press Enter. Click Finish.

   D. Right-click the server and select New ➤ Web Site. Type **Human Resources** and press Enter. Click Next. Click Next. Type **D:\HR** and press Enter. Click Finish.

Answers: B and **C.** A does not specify the path, D does not specify the IP address.

Write scripts to manage the FTP service or the WWW service.

Don't panic. You don't have to learn a scripting language to pass the IIS exam. In fact, although you can use scripting to manage services, you probably never will unless you're in the business of setting up Web sites full time. The purpose of this objective is merely to let you know that a scripting facility exists in IIS for the local machine and what functions can be automated through scripting.

NOTE   Refer to the IIS4 online documentation for more information about the Windows Scripting Host.

Critical Information

The Windows Scripting Host is a shell that allows you to use the VBScript and JScript interpreters (the very same ones used by Internet Explorer for browser-side scripting and IIS for server-side Active Server Pages) to control your server at the operating system level. The Windows Scripting Host is a shell or environment in which scripting languages run to gain access to the local machine's registry, file system, or other system services.

Scripting to Change Service Properties

You can use the Windows Scripting Host to write scripts that change the IIS service properties. For instance, if you implement Index Server on a system that already contains hundreds of Web sites, it might be easier to write a script to loop through all the sites and set the Index this directory setting than it would be to simply check the setting for each site. As you can see, you'd have to have a lot of sites in order to save time by writing a script instead of manually changing your sites.

Scripting to Create Web Sites

Creating Web sites is a much more practical purpose for the Windows Scripting Host. It is a relatively easy process to automatically generate customized Web sites with the Windows Scripting Host.

Say, for instance, you are a teacher, and you want to give your students their own Web sites for posting stories and scanned images that parents can browse from home. Setting up each site individually for every student every year would be very tedious indeed. You can use the Windows Scripting Host to create a directory for each student, create the Web site in IIS, create default HTML files for each student (modified to contain their names as the titles), and include default links and images. Students can then modify this default site to customize it any way they want. You can then use another script to remove the IIS Web site and archive the files and directories when the students leave your class at the end of the year.

Necessary Procedures

Use the following procedure to see how scripting can help you administer your Internet Server by creating Web sites:

1. Double-click My Computer and browse to `c:\winnt\system32\inetsrv\adminsamples`.

2. Right-click on the file named `mkw3site.vbs`.

3. View the Visual Basic code used to create a Web site.

4. Close the Notepad.

5. Select Start ➤ Programs ➤ Command prompt.

6. Type **cd c:\winnt\system32\inetsrv\adminsamples**.

7. Type **mkw3site.vbs -r c:\inetpub\wwwroot -t test -o 8085**.

8. Close the command prompt.

9. Launch the MMC.

10. Right-click on the test Web site and select Properties.

11. Verify that the port is set to 8085.

12. Delete the test Web site.

13. Close the MMC.

Exam Essentials

Understand the facility provided by scripting. The Windows Scripting Host provides the environment for scripting languages like JScript and VBScript to control the operating system and IIS itself. With this facility, you can automate repetitive tasks like creating Web sites and controlling services.

Key Terms and Concepts

Script: A text file containing commands in a specific syntax that can be interpreted to perform a certain function.

Scripting host: The environment in which a scripting language runs. The scripting host provides the objects that can be accessed by the scripting language to control the host environment. There are three scripting hosts provided with IIS: the Windows Scripting Host to control the operating system, Active Server Pages to automatically create HTML files and control the operation of IIS, and Internet Explorer, which interprets scripts on the client side.

Scripting language: A simple interpreted language used to control discrete programmatic functions. JScript and VBScript are both scripting languages, as are Perl and BASIC.

Sample Questions

1. Which of the following tasks is a poor choice for automating with a script?

A. Creating a large number of default Web sites for new users of a small ISP.

B. Starting and stopping intranet Web services automatically at night during backups.

C. Creating a wizard so that students can provide a few parameters to create their own Web sites.

D. Creating an e-magazine that showcases the talent of various short-story fiction writers on a Web site.

Answer: D. This problem doesn't require automation because it's only performed once.

Manage a Web site by using Content Analyzer. Tasks include:

- Creating, customizing, and navigating WebMaps
- Examining a Web site by using the various reports provided by Content Analyzer
- Tracking links by using a WebMap

Critical Information

Site Server Express Content Analyzer shows you how the Web pages on your site are related. It does not show you the pages themselves, and thus is similar to the Explorer (versus the Editor) in Microsoft FrontPage. You can use a regular browser to view the pages while using Content Analyzer, and you can specify which browser you will use to do so. You can also specify whether or not the Content Analyzer and Web browser should stay synchronized.

You can configure Content Analyzer to launch a helper application to view or edit any of the defined object types. This way you can use, for example, a text editor to fix a broken link or a paint tool to touch up a graphic image.

Each object type can have up to nine helpers defined for it. One use for this feature is to define several browsers with which to view a single Web page, thereby making sure that the page looks good in more than just Internet Explorer.

In Site Server Express you have two primary views of the Web site—a traditional, hierarchical view in the left panel and a cyberbolic view in the right panel. From this tab you can configure how the cyberbolic view will behave.

If the Web site you are mapping contains password-protected directories and you are accessing it via a URL, you will need to tell Site Server Express what those passwords are. Otherwise Site Server Express will not be able to map the password-protected portions of the Web site.

Creating a Web Map

A Web map is a graphical view of the resources in a Web site. When you create a Web map, Site Server Express traverses all of the HTML pages it can find in the Web site and records those pages as well as all of the objects (graphics, sounds, external pages, etc.) that those pages reference. The information about the Web site is stored in a .wmp file so that the Web site needn't be traversed every time you want to use Site Server Express. Site Server Express can traverse a Web site from URLs or from files. Figure 3.1 shows a cyberbolic Web map created in Content Analyzer.

F I G U R E 3.1: A cyberbolic WebMap

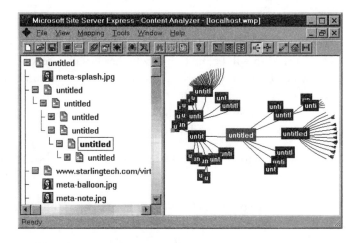

WebMaps from URLs

If Site Server Express is running on a different computer than IIS4, you will probably connect to the Web site using the Web site's URL. Site Server Express will use the HTTP protocol to connect to the site and gather its information.

When you create a WebMap, you can set constraints and options to limit how extensive your WebMap will be and hence how much space it will take up and how much of a load it will place on a remote (URL-accessed) Web site. In addition, you can instruct Site Server Express to make a local copy of the Web site.

In order to create a WebMap from a URL, you simply provide the URL path to the home page of the Web site. You can instruct Site Server Express to explore the entire site, to organize the WebMap by directory hierarchy rather than the order in which links are found, and to generate a site report automatically as it creates the WebMap. If you do not want Site Server Express to explore the entire site, you will be able to choose how many pages will be explored. When Site Server Express is done exploring the site, it will ask you for a name prefix for the summary report, and (if you instructed it to generate a report) show you summary statistics for the Web site.

WebMaps from Files

If the Web site is stored locally (either on the same computer as Site Server Express or on another computer in your LAN) you can point Site Server Express to the directory path or UNC path to the Web.

As with creating a URL-sourced WebMap, with a directly accessed Web site you can set constraints and options to limit how extensive your WebMap will be, including whether it will access off-site links and which URLs it will not explore. In addition, you can instruct Site Server Express to explore all of the content of the Web site directories, rather than just the content referenced by hyperlinks. This is an excellent way to find orphaned Web pages.

In order to create a WebMap from files, you must provide the following:

- a home page path and filename (this may be a UNC path or a standard pathname starting with a drive letter)

- a domain and site root (this may be the Internet name of the Web site)

- the location of the CGI Bin directory used by the Web site (specified the same way you specified the home page path and filename)

You can instruct Site Server Express to explore the entire site, to organize the WebMap by directory hierarchy (rather than the order in which links are found), and to generate a site report automatically as it creates the WebMap. If you do not want Site Server Express to explore the entire site, you will be able to choose how many pages will be explored. When Site Server Express is done exploring the site, it will ask you for a name prefix for the summary report and (if you instructed it to generate a report) show you summary statistics for the Web site.

Configuring WebMaps

By clicking on the Options... button in the New Map from URL window, you get a new panel with four tabs:

General From this tab you specify the creation and exploration options of Site Server Express, including:

Ignore Case of URLs Some operating systems (such as Windows NT) do not differentiate between uppercase and lowercase letters in filenames. Other operating systems (such as UNIX) do. You should set this option to match how the operating system hosting the Web site treats filename case.

Ignore Default WebMaps (URL WebMaps) You can configure IIS4 (and other Web servers as well) to provide a default Web map to Site Server when Site Server begins to explore a site. Retrieving a locally stored Web map takes considerably less time and generates less Web server load than creating a new Web map. The default Web map may not be current, however, or may not include all of the information you require.

If No Default File, Map All Files in Directory (file WebMaps) Some links may point to a directory rather than a file, and if directory browsing is allowed for that directory you may want the contents of the directory to be mapped as well.

Verify Offsite Links Check this option if you want to make sure that links to other Web sites are still valid.

Honor Robot Protocol Some Web sites have areas marked off-limits to automated Web index creators (commonly called Web spiders or Web crawlers). You can configure Site Server Express to not explore those areas on the site you are indexing.

User Agent (URL-based) In this field you specify the user agent Site Server Express will use to explore the site. Your choices are Microsoft, Mozilla 2.0, or Mozilla 3.0. (Mozilla is the development name for Netscape Navigator.)

Local Site Root Directory (file-based) If you move the location of the Web site, you can change this setting to match.

Site Copy You use this tab to copy a Web site from the Web server to your local hard drive. You must specify the directory location where you want the copy to be stored.

Extensions From this tab you specify what additional Web sites on your server Site Server Express will explore. The settings are as follows:

None Site Server Express will only explore from the root you have specified and subroots below it.

All Other Domains All references to pages or resources on the Web site, including those laterally and closer to the root, will be explored by Site Server Express. For example, if you start exploring at `www.mysite.com/mainsite/start/home` `.html` and the page `www.mysite.com/mainsite/start/` `details/summary.html` has a reference to `www.mysite.com/` `mainsite/graphics.html`, then the graphics domain will be explored as well.

Auto Explore URLs Starting With This option allows you to specify particular domains (relative URL paths) that Site Server Express will explore.

Restrictions From this tab you specify which URL paths Site Server Express will not explore.

Using WebMap Summary Reports

Site Server Express creates a summary report for you automatically (unless you tell it not to) and displays it in your Web browser when you create an initial WebMap. Microsoft Site Server (the commercial version, which is not included with Internet Information Server 4) has additional reports that can tell you more about your Web site. The summary report is divided into three parts:

Object Statistics This part lists the number and size of the objects stored in your Web site, broken down by their type (such as HTML pages, Java classes, image files, and so on).

Status Summary This part describes the links in your Web site, separated into on-site and off-site links, and shows the number of good links, bad links, missing links, and unverified links.

Map Statistics This part gives you such information as when the map was made, how "deep" it got, and the average number of links on a page in the Web site.

Searching the Links

A graphic view of your Web links is a neat tool, but the real benefit of Site Server Express is its ability to search your Web site for problems such as broken links, "not found" objects, images without ALT tags, and large objects (which can cause a page to take a very long time to download). The Tools menu gives you the option to do a quick search on the following objects:

- Broken Links
- Home Site Objects
- Images Without ALT
- Load Size over 32K
- Non-Home Site Objects
- Not Found Objects (404)
- Unavailable Objects
- Unverified Objects

When you search on any one of these objects, Site Server Express creates a search results window and lists those objects in it. When you click on the object in the search results window, the tree view and cyberbolic view automatically go to that object. You can then double-click on the object (or its parent if it is a broken link or a not-found object) to view the problem object or HTML page.

Site Server Express makes finding broken links easy. Then it is just a matter of fixing that link with the software you used to create the page, or perhaps just editing the file with a text editor, so that the link points to the correct location. You need to set Verify offsite links if you want Site Server Express to make sure links outside your site valid, because it does not verify them by default.

NOTE Site Server Express, unfortunately, does not give you the capability to search for user-defined text, including searching for the content of hypertext links, headings, or titles. If you want to search for these items you must purchase Site Analyst. Site Analyst is a feature of Microsoft Site Server 2 and Microsoft Site Server, Enterprise Edition 2.

Necessary Procedures

Creating, Customizing, and Navigating WebMaps

The following procedure will show you how to create a WebMap from a file location. Creating them from URLs is a similar process.

1. Select Start ➤ Programs ➤ Administrative Tools ➤ Windows NT 4 Option Pack ➤ Site Server Express 2.0 ➤ Content Analyzer to start the Content Analyzer.

2. Click the New WebMap button.

3. Select File and click OK.

4. Enter the home page path and filename of the default Web site home page (`C:\InetPub\wwwroot\index.htm` for most installations).

5. Enter the domain site and root (the name of your server).

6. Enter the location of the Scripts directory for the location of the CGI Bin directory (`C:\InetPub\Scripts` for most installations).

7. Click OK.

8. Click OK in the Generate Site Reports window.

9. Observe the Server Summary report and then close the report (browser) window.

10. Select View ➤ Program Options.

11. Click the Cyberbolic tab.

12. Check the Enable Snap Mode option.

13. Uncheck the Show Common Ancestor When Selecting in Tree View option.

14. Click Apply.

15. Click OK.

Examining a Web Site by Using the Various Reports Provided by Content Analyzer

Content Analyzer for Site Server Express does not create various reports, it creates only one: the Site Summary report. You've already seen this report in the previous exercise, but you can use the following procedure to call it up again at any time:

1. Launch Internet Explorer.

2. Point to the file created in the previous procedure. By default this file is `C:\Program Files\Content Analyzer Express\Reports\localhost_summary.html`.

3. View the statistics presented in the HTML file.

4. Close Internet Explorer.

Tracking Links by Using a WebMap

WebMaps make browsing the links in your Web site easy. Use the following procedure to track links using a WebMap:

1. Select Start ➤ Programs ➤ Administrative Tools ➤ Windows NT 4 Option Pack ➤ Site Server Express 2.0 ➤ Content Analyzer to start the Content Analyzer.

2. Click the Open WebMap button.

3. Select the file you created in the previous procedure and click OK.

4. In the cyberbolic view pane, click the various links to track through the HTML links in your Web site.

5. Right-click on a page with many links and select Links.

6. View the link statistics.

7. Click OK.

8. Close Content Analyzer.

Exam Essentials

Understand the purpose of Content Analyzer.   Content Analyzer maps out your Web site to provide statistics and a graphical view you can use to track down broken links and quickly find Web pages.

Know the difference between mapping a site via the file system and mapping via URLs.   When analyzing sites from files, Content Analyzer can scan files that are not linked to the default page, thus showing orphaned pages.

Key Terms and Concepts

Cyberbolic: A shape that changes its form to match the data that it displays in real-time.

WebMap: A cyberbolic map of a Web site that graphically shows pages connected by the links contained in them.

Sample Questions

1. You want to make sure that you have no broken links, either to locations inside your Web site or to other Web servers on the Internet. Which option should you check?

   A. Honor Robot Protocol

   B. Verify Offsite Links

   C. User Agent

   D. Ignore Case of URLs

   Answer: B. By default, Content Analyzer will not verify the integrity of links outside your Web site.

2. You want to use Content Analyzer to map a Web site that contains password-protected Web pages. The pages are in a directory that has only Windows NT Challenge/Response enabled. Content Analyzer fails to map those pages when you make the map using a URL. What is the problem?

   A. You must enable the "Allow Content Analyzer to Scan Directory" permission in the Web site's Properties panel.

   B. You must enable Basic Authentication for that directory.

   C. You must enable Secure Socket Layer communications for that directory.

   D. You must provide a correct default domain for basic authentication in the Web directory Security tab for that directory.

   Answer: B. Site Server Express uses Basic Authentication to connect to password-secured resources via a URL.

Configure Microsoft SMTP Service to host message traffic.

The Simple Mail Transfer Protocol (SMTP) service provided with IIS4 gives you the ability to mail-enable your Web sites. Using the SMTP service, you can send mail from a Web page and receive e-mail to a general delivery mailbox on your Web server.

Critical Information

The SMTP service provides the function of sending and routing mail. You can use it to create mail messages that are then forwarded to e-mail recipients on the Web. You can also use SMTP to provide a mail relay function and to receive mail to a general delivery directory on your server.

NOTE The SMTP service provided with IIS4 does not support the use of individual mailboxes for users, nor does it provide a POP3 or MAPI service to allow clients to check their mail. It is provided only to mail-enable Web sites. You'll have to use another product, such as Microsoft Exchange Server or one of the many excellent POP server products for Windows NT, if you want mail for your own Internet users.

The directories listed in Table 3.5 are installed in the mailroot directory. These directories manage all of the e-mail handling provided by the SMTP service. The online documentation provides more information about using text files as an interface to the mail system.

T A B L E 3.5:   Default Mail Folders

Folder	Description
Badmail	Holds undeliverable mail that could not be returned to the sender.
Drop	Receives all incoming mail for the domain. You can choose any directory to be the drop directory except the pickup directory.
Pickup	Processes outgoing text messages that are copied to the directory.
Queue	Holds messages for delivery when they can't be immediately delivered.

Another method of sending mail is to connect to port 25 on the mail host and transmit the text of the message. This is easy using programming languages like Java that can establish socket connections in a single line of code. You can simulate this usage by using the Telnet utility to attach to port 25 and typing in an e-mail message.

SMTP Service Specifics

The Messages panel, accessed by right-clicking on the SMTP service and selecting Properties, allows you to set specific parameters relating to message delivery for the SMTP service. Figure 3.2 shows the SMTP service Properties panel.

Here you can control the size of messages, the maximum session size, the number of messages per connection, maximum recipients, and undeliverable message handling.

Maximum message size is the preferred limit for the server. A message exceeding this size will still be transmitted as long as it's smaller than the maximum session size.

FIGURE 3.2: SMTP Properties

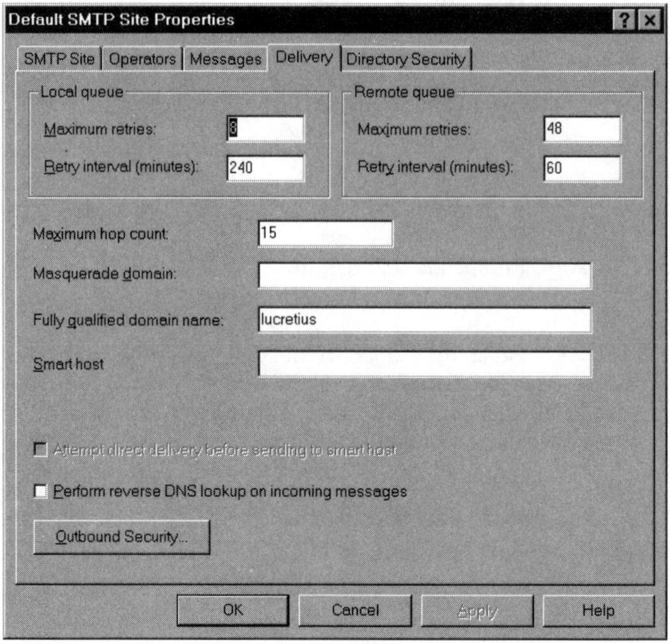

TIP Familiarize yourself with the process of SMTP message size limiting.

Maximum session size is the absolute maximum size a message can be. If a message exceeds this size, the connection will be dropped immediately. The connecting mail host is likely to retry the connection up to its retry limit, so setting this value too low will result in a lot of wasted network bandwidth.

Maximum number of outbound messages per connection allows you to specify how many messages will be transmitted per connection. When the number of messages transmitted exceeds the value of this parameter, the existing connection is used, but a new connection is automatically opened. This can improve performance in cases where more than one physical path to the remote hosts exists. By setting a reasonably low number, you can force the creation of numerous simultaneous connections in parallel, which (if the bandwidth exists) will be faster than a single serial connection.

Maximum number of recipients per message specifies how many recipients are permitted per connection. If a message exceeds the number of recipients specified by this parameter, a new connection will be created to handle the additional recipients.

Send a copy of non-delivery reports to allows you to specify an e-mail address that you want copies of non-deliverable messages sent to. This allows you to track the accuracy of the e-mail addresses specified.

Badmail directory allows you to specify the directory where messages that were not deliverable are stored.

Delivery options specify exactly how the connections used to transmit messages are handled. This panel controls retries, maximum hops, domain name settings, and smart host settings. A smart host is a host to which all outbound mail can be transmitted for further delivery.

Local/Remote queue Maximum retries specifies the number of times the SMTP service will attempt to deliver a message from the local queue. Once this limit is reached, the message is sent to the Badmail directory and a non-delivery report is generated.

Local/Remote queue Retry interval (minutes) specifies the time between retry attempts.

Maximum hop count specifies the number of SMTP hosts the message can travel through before it is dropped. The primary purpose of this counter is to prevent circular message paths, because most mail is transmitted with very few intervening servers.

Masquerade domain allows you to specify a domain name other than the domain name of the machine transmitting the mail to be placed in the From and Mail From fields of the message.

Fully qualified domain name can be used to specify a domain name other than the local host's domain name.

Smart host can be used to specify another SMTP server that you want all mail from the local host routed to directly. You'll use this option when a less costly path exists, or when you are downstream from an Internet Service Provider that provides an SMTP relay server that you want to use. Often, transmitting to a relay server on a faster pipe will improve performance.

Attempt direct delivery before sending to smart host allows you to specify that the local host is to attempt a direct connection to the receiving host and to transmit to the smart host only if the connection attempt fails. This puts the retry burden on the smart host.

Perform reverse DNS lookup on incoming messages forces the SMTP service to look up the domain name of the transmitting server and make sure it matches the domain name in the From and Mail From fields of the message—thus preventing mail forgery. Unfortunately, reverse DNS lookups put quite a burden on your mail host, and many legitimate mail servers use masquerade domains.

Outbound Security allows you to specify both logon security and encryption settings for remote hosts. Normally, you'll use these settings when you transmit to a smart host or other machine that you control. Most Internet mail hosts do not use encryption or logon security.

No Authentication specifies that no authentication is to be performed.

Clear text authentication specifies that a normal user logon is required to transmit mail.

Windows NT Challenge/Response authentication and encryption specifies that an NT-compatible challenge and response authentication must take place. This setting works only with other Windows NT mail hosts.

TLS encryption specifies that transport layer security encryption is to be used.

Basic SMTP site security is controlled through the Directory Security panel. This panel gives you several options for controlling access to your SMTP server.

Anonymous access and authentication control allows you to specify the authentication required by users who will access the SMTP directories. You can chose from Allow Anonymous Access, Basic Authentication, or Windows NT Challenge/Response as appropriate for your site.

Secure communications allows you to require the level of security that inbound connections must conform to for your SMTP site. Options are Require a secure channel and Require 128 bit encryption. You can also launch the Key Manager by clicking the button on this panel.

IP Address and Domain Name Restrictions allows you to restrict access to the SMTP site by IP address, a block of IP addresses, or by domain name. This restriction works the same way address-based restrictions work for the other services.

Relay Restrictions allows you to restrict the servers you'll let relay mail to your SMTP site. You can grant access to specific hosts, and you can grant relay access to any host that can authenticate successfully.

The SMTP service is configured automatically to support one default domain. You can add aliases to the service so that the SMTP service can handle mail destined for those domain names. There are two types of domains:

- **Local domains** route mail to the drop directory on the local host. You'll use local domains when you need to specify another domain name for your mail server.

- **Remote domains** route mail to other SMTP hosts. You'll configure remote domains when you need to override your default SMTP site authentication, encryption, and smart host settings for a specific domain.

TIP Be sure you know how to create remote SMTP domains.

Domain settings are very simple. From the Domain Settings panel you have the following options:

Local/Remote determines whether the alias is local to this host or a remote host.

Default specifies that this is the domain name for the default directory.

Alias specifies that this domain is an alias.

Drop directory specifies the location of the drop directory. You can use any local directory except the pickup directory as a drop directory.

Route domain specifies an SMTP host that all mail for this domain should be routed to.

Allow incoming mail to be relayed to this domain is self-explanatory.

Outbound security allows you to set authentication and encryption settings to attach to this remote domain. These settings can be used to override the SMTP default settings for a specific domain.

Necessary Procedures

Use the following procedure to create a remote SMTP domain that overrides your default security for a specific mail recipient:

1. Launch the MMC.

2. Expand the default SMTP Site.

3. Right-click on the default SMTP Site and select New ➤ Domain.

4. Select Remote in the Domain Type radio button group and click Next.

5. Enter **test** in the Name to be used for the new domain input box and click Finish.

6. Right-click on the test domain and select Properties.

7. Enter footest.com in the Route domain input box.

8. Click the Outbound Security button.

9. Check TLS encryption.

10. Click OK.

11. Click OK.

12. Close the MMC.

Exam Essentials

Understand the purpose of SMTP. SMTP transmits, receives, and relays mail messages between servers. It does not separate mail messages into mailboxes or provide a specific interface for users to retrieve e-mail messages.

Know how to manage the SMTP service. Understand how to change common SMTP service settings like message size restrictions, logging, and retry timings.

Key Terms and Concepts

E-mail: An addressed text message that is transmitted through a series of mail servers until it reaches its destination domain, where it is stored until retrieved by the intended recipient user.

Masquerade domain: A name placed in the From field of an outbound e-mail message that is different than the domain name of the server actually originating the mail.

Simple Mail Transfer Protocol (SMTP): A TCP/IP protocol that transfers e-mail between hosts.

Smart host: A mail server to which all outbound mail is transmitted and all inbound mail is received. A mail proxy.

Sample Questions

1. You've noticed performance degradation on your IIS machine because anonymous users are posting e-mail messages to non-existent addresses. Configure SMTP retry/timeout to retry a maximum of eight times and delay 240 minutes between attempts for the local host. Choose the correct method:

    A. Right-click on the SMTP site, select Properties, select Messages, enter **8** in the Maximum Retries input box, enter **240** in the Retry Interval input box, click OK.

    B. Right-click on the SMTP site, select Properties, enter **8** in the Maximum Retries input box, enter **240** in the Retry Interval input box, click OK.

    C. Right-click on the SMTP site, select Properties, select Service Properties, enter **8** in the Maximum Retries input box, enter **240** in the Retry Interval input box, click OK.

    D. Right-click on the SMTP site, select Properties, select Delivery, enter **8** in the Maximum Retries input box, enter **240** in the Retry Interval input box, click OK.

    Answer: D. Other options won't work.

2. You have a 56K connection to the Internet. You've noticed that some very large files are being sent to your SMTP server by clients who are attaching pictures to their mail messages. You want to reject e-mail messages larger than 32K. Choose the method that will enable you to close connections when messages are too large:

    A. Select Default SMTP Site, select Action ➤ Properties, select Messages, enter **32** in the Maximum Message Size input box.

    B. Select Default SMTP Site, select Action ➤ Properties, select Messages, enter **32** in the Maximum Session Size input box.

    C. Select Default SMTP Site, select Action ➤ Properties, select Delivery, enter **32** in the Maximum Message Size input box.

    D. Select Default SMTP Site, select Action ➤ Properties, select Delivery, enter **32** in the Maximum Session Size input box.

Answer: B. Although A appears correct, the Microsoft SMTP service will still allow messages larger than the size specified there. Using a maximum session size, the connection will be dropped immediately if the message is larger than the size specified. C and D don't work.

Configure Microsoft NNTP Service to host a newsgroup.

NNTP is a client/server public bulletin board service. News hosts store a hierarchical database of news messages by newsgroup or topic. Users may post new messages to a newsgroup, create a new newsgroup, or view the messages in a newsgroup using a news client like Internet Mail and News or Outlook Express, which come with different versions of Internet Explorer. Many companies use NNTP to create newsgroups based on projects and clients and then simply refer to these newsgroups to post information or check facts about the project. News is primarily a collaboration tool.

Critical Information

NNTP configuration is performed by right-clicking on the NNTP service in the scope pane of the Microsoft Management Console and setting options in the various panels.

News Site allows you to specify a site description for the MMC, a path header to be used in the path line of each news posting, the IP address and TCP ports the service responds to, connection limitations, and logging options. See the corresponding panels in the sections on WWW, FTP, or SMTP service for more information.

Security Accounts allows you to specify the anonymous account to use for NNTP and the NNTP service operators. See the corresponding panels in the sections on WWW, FTP, or SMTP service for more information.

NNTP Settings allows you to configure how the service responds to NNTP requests.

Allow Client Posting enables posts from clients to this news site. Unless you allow client posting, your news site will be read-only.

Allow Servers to Pull News Articles from This Server allows other news servers to replicate news articles from this server.

Allow Control Messages lets you determine whether control messages should be automatically processed.

SMTP Server for Moderated Groups specifies the SMTP server where moderated messages are forwarded. Optionally, this can be a local directory path on the local machine.

Default Moderator Domain specifies the mail domain for moderated messages. Moderated messages are sent to *newsgroupname@defaultdomain*. You must have e-mail accounts set up on that domain to receive moderated messages.

Administrator Email Account specifies the e-mail account to which non-delivery reports are sent when mail cannot be delivered to a moderator.

Home Directory lets you configure how the service stores the news files.

Directory Location and **Local Path** specify the location of the home directory as per the other services.

Allow Posting is analogous to the Allow Write Access option for the other services. For public news forums, this option is generally left on. For support bulletins, this option is generally turned off.

Restrict Newsgroup Visibility allows you to use NTFS permissions and authenticated logons to restrict the visibility of newsgroups to permitted users. This option creates considerable overhead and should not be used for sites that generally use anonymous access.

Log Access is the same as for other services.

Index News Contents allows Index Server to index newsgroups. This setting is set in the Home Directory for all newsgroups and can be changed for virtual directories.

Secure Communications operates the same as for the other services.

Directory Security is similar to the Directory Security panel for the WWW and FTP services.

Groups allows you to control how newsgroups are set up. This is a complex option so it is discussed separately in the next section.

Controlling Newsgroups

From the Groups tab you configure the topics of discussion as follows:

Create New Newsgroup allows you to create a newsgroup. This option opens a Newsgroups Properties dialog box. Creating a newsgroup immediately creates a directory in the `c:\inetpub\ nntpfile\root` directory with the same name as the newsgroup. Posts for that newsgroup are stored in that directory.

Newsgroup Finder allows you to search for newsgroups based on search criteria.

Edit opens a Newsgroup Properties dialog box for the newsgroup you select in the Matching newsgroups list box.

Delete deletes the newsgroup selected in the Matching newsgroups list box. Files and directories from deleted newsgroups are removed the next time the service is stopped.

The Newsgroups Properties dialog box has the following controls:

Newsgroup specifies the name of the newsgroup.

Description describes the newsgroup in further detail.

Newsgroup Prettyname can contain Unicode characters for other languages that some news clients support.

Read only allows you to prevent posts to the newsgroup.

Moderation options specify by whom the newsgroup is moderated: Not moderated, Moderated by default newsgroup moderator, Moderated by the e-mail account specified.

Virtual NNTP Directories

As with the other services, you can create virtual directories that appear as newsgroups in your NNTP service. The purpose of virtual directories in NNTP is to make content appear as though it is a normal subdirectory of your NNTP home directory when in fact it is located in another path, on another volume, or on another computer. The process for creating and using virtual directories with NNTP is the same as for Web and FTP sites.

Necessary Procedures

Use the following procedure to create a normal moderated newsgroup:

1. Launch the MMC.

2. Right-click Default NNTP Site and select Properties.

3. Select the Groups tab.

4. Click Create New Newsgroup.

5. Enter **testing** in the newsgroup name input box.

6. Enter **A Test Newsgroup** in the Description input box.

7. Select Moderated By and enter your e-mail address in the input box.

8. Click OK.

9. Click OK.

Exam Essentials

Know how NNTP virtual directories work. NNTP virtual directories are similar to virtual directories in the WWW and FTP services, but because the newsgroup structure of your site matches the directory hierarchy, their exact location in the directory tree may be more important.

Know how to enable NNTP site indexing by Index Server. Enable indexing of NNTP content by checking the Index News Content checkbox in the Home Directory Properties panel.

Know how to configure NNTP service settings for functions such as logging. Browse through all the configuration settings in the NNTP Properties panel. Make sure you know how to control all the various features presented.

Key Terms and Concepts

Moderator: A person who determines which posts should become part of a newsgroup. Moderators are e-mailed the text of each post, and can either delete or return the post.

Newsgroup: A body of posts related by topic. Newsgroups are hierarchically related.

NNTP: A TCP/IP service that allows the browsing of newsgroups, displays the posts contained therein, and receives new posts to be added to the newsgroups.

Post: A public message hosted by the NNTP protocol.

Sample Questions

1. Users of your intranet NNTP site want to be able to search for newsgroup posts based on a keyword. What's the best way to support this functionality?

   A. Post the newsgroups on a Web site. Have Index Server index the Web site.

   B. Enable NNTP Index Server searches in the NNTP configuration snap-in.

   C. Configure Index Server to search the NNTP directories by making them virtual directories in the Web service.

   D. Convert all posts to MS-Word documents and store them in a directory searched by Index Server.

   Answer: B. All these methods will probably work, but B is the simplest.

Configure Certificate Server to issue certificates.

Certificate Server allows you to create the digital certificates necessary to establish secure connections over the Internet. You'll use Certificate Server whenever you want to secure your Web sites for commercial purposes.

SEE ALSO Refer to *NT Network Security* by Matthew Strebe, Charles Perkins, and Michael Moncur (Sybex, 1998) for more information about security and encryption.

Critical Information

Installing Certificate Server is easy. In fact, you installed Certificate Server along with IIS, Index Server, and many other Windows NT Option Pack components in Chapter 1. Everything you need to configure for Certificate Server is completed during the setup phase.

Using Certificate Server is also automatic. You don't need to do anything specific with it to generate SSL keys. The following process should demystify what's going on with Certificate Server, the Key Manager, and SSL:

1. Install Certificate Server.

2. Use Key Manager to generate key requests. These requests are automatically fulfilled by Certificate Server if you have it installed.

3. Insert the key into the Web site. At this point, Certificate Server and Key Manager are no longer necessary unless you want to create additional SSL certificates.

4. Enable SSL security encryption on the Web page using the Management Console.

Using the Key Manager

The use of Secure Socket Layer communications requires keys, and you use the Key Manager to create them and install them in a Web site. You can start the Key Manager from the Directory Security tab of a Web site or virtual directory Properties window (it will run automatically when you click the Key Manager button if you don't already have a key installed in your Web site).

Connecting to Servers and Viewing Keys

You can use Key Manager to manage the keys of several servers. When you start the Key Manager program, you will see the WWW server(s) on the local computer. You connect to additional servers using the Connect to Machine option on the Server menu.

The Key Manager main window has two panels. The left side shows the WWW servers you are connected to and the keys that are configured for those servers. You can expand or collapse the view of a particular server or computer by clicking the plus sign next to the computer or WWW entry.

The right side of the window details a selected key. You can see the key's name, its status, the range of time it is valid for, and the distinguishing information for the key that you entered during key creation (see Figure 3.3).

When you double-click the key or select Properties from the Key menu, you see the Server Connection information for that key. This window specifies how your Web server uses the key. From this window you configure which IP address and port number combinations this certificate will be used for. If the window is empty, the certificate will not be used. You can add an entry that specifies that the key will be used for any port and any IP address, or you can be more specific (limiting the key to a particular port, IP address, or both).

F I G U R E 3.3: The Key Manager program is where you create keys and install certificates for the WWW service.

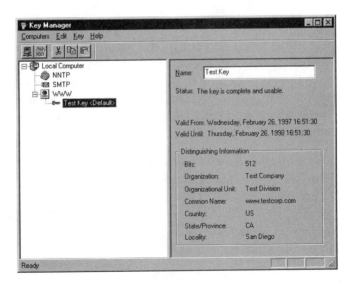

Generating Keys

You generate keys from the Create New Key menu option of the Key menu. (Select a WWW server to contain the key first.) The key name and the password identify the key. The Bits field sets the strength of the key. (Depending on the version of your security DLLs, you may be limited to 512 bits or you may be able to select a more secure length such as 1024 or greater bits.) The key will be either placed in a file you specify or sent automatically to your Certificate Server.

The Distinguishing Information fields in the middle of the window describe your organization. This information, plus the identity of your Web server, is what the certificate authority will be "signing."

If you see a key with a slash through it, the key still requires a certificate. In order to make the key complete and usable, you must send the key to a certificate authority. You can send your request to various certificate authorities, or you can use the Certificate Server software to be your own certificate authority. The certificate authority mentioned in the Microsoft Help information is VeriSign. (You can visit the VeriSign Web site at http://www.verisign.com/microsoft/ for more information.)

If you are using the Certificate Server as your certificate authority, your key will then be complete and usable. You will want to select which IP and port addresses you will use the key for (or you can set it to all ports and IP addresses).

If you are not using Certificate Server for this function, after you submit the request to the certificate authority (usually via e-mail, with other information and perhaps a fee sent by other means) you should receive a file containing a certificate you can install in the key you created. You install a certificate (in the form of a text file) by selecting Install Key Certificate from the Key menu and selecting the file that contains the certificate. You will have to enter the password for the key. After you do so, your key's status will change to complete and usable. You will then be able to require Secure Socket Layer on directories in your WWW service. Instructions for how to install a certificate in your Web site are given below.

Moving, Importing, and Exporting Keys

Once you have installed a key, you can move the key between WWW servers using the cut, copy, and paste options in the Edit menu. You can also export the key to a backup file and import the key from a backup file or a keyset file. (Some security programs that create and manage keys store those keys in keysets, which are special files on the hard disk.)

Necessary Procedures

There is no specific method to enable Certificate Server: once it's installed, it's running and enabled. Use the following procedure to install a digital certificate on your Web Site:

1. Right-click on the Web site you want to install a certificate on and select Properties.

2. Click the Directory Security tab.

3. Click the Key Manager button.

4. Right-click the WWW service and select Create New Key....

5. Accept Automatically Send the Request to an On-Line Authority and click the Next button.

6. Enter **test key** in the Key Name field.

7. Enter **test** in the Password field.

8. Enter **test** again in the Confirm Password field.

9. Click the Next button.

10. Enter **test company** in the Organization field.

11. Enter **test division** in the Organizational Unit field.

12. Enter the fully qualified domain name that will be used by Web browsers to access the Web site in the Common Name field (e.g., www.footest.com).

13. Click the Next button.

14. Enter your country in the Country field.

15. Enter your state or province in the State/Province field.

16. Enter your city or locality in the City/Locality field.

17. Click the Finish button. (The certificate will be automatically submitted to the Certificate Server on your IIS computer if you installed Certificate Server as instructed in Chapter 1.)

18. Click the Add... button.

19. Accept the Any Unassigned IP Address and Any Unassigned Port options and click the OK button.

20. Click the OK button again.

21. Select Commit Changes Now from the Computers menu.

22. Select Exit from the Computers menu.

23. In the Properties tab for the Test Web site, click the Secure Communications Edit... button again.

24. Check the Require Secure Channel When Using This Resource button.

25. Click the OK button.

26. Click the Apply button.

27. Click the OK button.

Exam Essentials

Understand the process for generating certificates and the role of Certificate Server.   Certificate requests are generated by the Key Manager, and fulfilled by the Certificate Server. Once you've generated a key and installed it into IIS, you can require Secure Socket Layer.

Key Terms and Concepts

Certificate: A one-way encrypted hash that can be decrypted to prove the identity of the sender without providing the ability to forge the hash. Certificates are thus used as "digital signatures" to authorize transactions and prove identities in the absence of physical proof.

Sample Questions

1. What tool do you use to generate keys?

   A. User Manager

   B. Key Manager

   C. Certificate Server

   D. Microsoft Management Console

Answer: B. The Certificate Server digitally signs keys created by the Key Manager.

Configure Index Server to index a Web site.

Index Server enhances IIS by providing a method to search for documents like Web pages or office documents (or any other document type with an installed content filter) on a server by keyword rather than by name. Index Server creates a database of words contained in documents that are stored on the server. You can then simply enter a plain language search phrase, and Index Server will return a list of documents that satisfy the search phrase. Search phrases are called queries in database and indexing parlance.

SEE ALSO More detailed information on the operation of Index Server is available in *MCSE: Internet Information Server 4 Study Guide* by Matthew Strebe and Charles Perkins (Sybex, 1998).

Critical Information

Index Server is administered and queried through the Index Server MMC snap-in or through the HTML Index Server manager. The HTML pages you include in your Web site to allow users to query Index Server are called Query HTML pages. Index Server can index any type of document that you've installed a content filter for. Content filters are plug-ins that Index Server uses to read a specific type of file. Index Server comes with content filters for HTML and for the Microsoft Office applications. Index Server cannot index documents for which there is no installed content filter.

Index Server doesn't necessarily search your entire site. It searches only the virtual directories you specify, which by default is your entire site. This feature allows you to remove virtual directories that you don't want indexed. You specify whether you want a site or virtual directory indexed by checking the Index this directory option in the Home Directory Properties panel.

You may need to have more than one catalog if you have more than one Web site on your server. Each Web site should have its own catalog to prevent documents contained on one site from showing up on queries in another. Queries cannot span more than one catalog. You create a new catalog by right-clicking on the Web object in the Index Server snap-in and selecting New ➤ Directory.

Index servers can open an interesting security loophole. Since the index process runs as a system process, it has higher security access to documents on the server than many logged-on users have. Therefore, a query issued to an index server could return fragments of files that the user does not have permission to access—thus alerting the user to the presence of the document and possibly revealing segments of sensitive information.

Index Server prevents this situation by automatically cataloging the ACL for each file it indexes. When a user issues a query, each document that satisfies the query (called a query hit) is checked against the user's permissions. If the user would not normally have permission to view the document, the query is removed from the results list and no indication of the document's existence is revealed.

You can use a single Index Server to index multiple Web sites in your NT security domain by simply sharing the site and creating a virtual root for it on your machine. This requires creating a custom .htx file to return the correct link because the path to the HTTP document will be different between the two machines. The online product documentation discusses this problem and its solution in detail.

Indexing across NT domain boundaries is more complex. To successfully use Index servers in other domains, follow these steps:

1. Establish trust relationships such that the NT domains containing servers to be indexed trust the NT domain in which the indexing server resides.

2. Establish a user account that has the authority to access files on the remote servers. This account must have the 'interactive logon' right to log on locally to each Web server to be indexed.

3. Stop and start the Content Index service to begin indexing the remote machines once they've been configured.

4. Share and set up directories to be indexed as virtual directories on the indexing server.

TIP   Make sure you know the security requirements to allow inter-domain Index Server access.

Necessary Procedures

Use the following procedure to enable indexing on a Web site from the MMC:

1. Right-click on the Web site and select Properties.
2. Select the Home Directory tab.
3. Check Index this directory.
4. Click OK.

Exam Essentials

Know how to index specific Web sites.   You enable indexing of a Web site by checking the Index this site checkbox in the Home Directory tab of a Web site or the Index this directory checkbox in a virtual directory.

Know how to create new catalogs and understand the scope of a catalog.   You create new catalogs by right-clicking on the Web object of the Index Server snap-in. Catalogs span across all virtual directories in the Web site as long as the virtual directories have the Index this directory checkbox checked.

Know the security requirements to allow interdomain Index Server access.   To successfully index across domains, you must establish an interdomain trust relationship and a user account with the security permissions to access the data that you want indexed.

Key Terms and Concepts

Catalog: The indexing data maintained by Index Server that contains the word list and the documents in which those words exist.

Corpus: The body of documents indexed by Index Server.

Index: The process of cataloging the location of words in a body of documents for cross-referencing.

Query: The process of retrieving documents based on the presence of specific keywords in the body of the document.

Sample Questions

1. You've established a single Index Server for your company that actually searches four different Web servers. Index Server won't return pages for the two Web servers on different domains. What should you do? (Choose all correct answers.)

   A. Establish trust relationships between the domains.

   B. Establish a user account with the necessary permissions to scan directories in the other domains.

   C. Stop and start the Content Index service.

   D. Add virtual directories that match the Web shares on the remote machines.

   Answer: A, B, C, and **D.** All these steps are necessary for inter-domain indexing.

2. Choose the answer that describes the steps necessary to create a new catalog called Documents that filters files on the entire D:\ drive on your Web server, assuming the Management Console is already running and the Index Server snap-in is loaded:

   A. Select Console Root on Local Machine, select Action ➤ New ➤ Catalog, enter **Documents** in the name field, enter D:\ in the Path Field, click OK, click OK to dismiss the offline warning.

   B. Select Index Server on Local Machine, select Action ➤ New ➤ Catalog, enter **Documents** in the name field, enter D:\ in the Path Field, click OK, click OK to dismiss the offline warning.

   C. Expand Index Server on Local Machine, select Web, select Action ➤ New ➤ Directory, enter D:\ in the Path Field, enter **Documents** in the Alias field, click OK.

D. Expand Index Server on Local Machine, select Web, select Action ➤ New ➤ Catalog, enter **Documents** in the name field, enter **D:** in the Path Field, click OK.

Answer: B. Other options either don't work or result in a new virtual directory rather than a new catalog.

3. Which answer describes the steps necessary to delete the default catalog, assuming the Management Console is already running and the Index Server snap-in is loaded?

   A. Select Index Server on Local Machine, select Action ➤ Stop, select Action ➤ Delete.

   B. Select Index Server on Local Machine, select Action ➤ Stop, Expand Index Server on Local Machine, Expand Web, select Directories, select `c:\inetpub\wwwroot` (or its equivalent on your machine), select Action ➤ Delete.

   C. Select Index Server on Local Machine, select Action ➤ Stop, Expand Index Server on Local Machine, select Web, select Action ➤ Delete.

   D. Expand Index Server on Local Machine, select Web, select Action ➤ Delete ➤ Catalog, click OK.

   Answer: C. Other options either are impossible or don't delete the catalog.

Manage MIME types.

Multimedia Internet Mail Extensions (MIME) are used by Web servers to inform Web browsers what type of information is being sent so that the Web browser can select the proper plug-in to interpret it. For example, when sending audio data to a Web browser, the server must inform the browser that the audio player plug-in should be used or the content will be displayed as garbage on the screen.

Critical Information

MIME types are necessary because not all computers use the same file naming conventions and because filenames are not transmitted from the server to the browser. MIME types consist of File Extension/MIME Type pairs. When a browser connects to your server and requests a file with a specific extension, the Web server checks that extension against its MIME type list and returns the MIME type of the data before the data stream begins. The browser then selects the plug-in that handles that type of content and provides the data stream to it.

To add a MIME type to support some new plug-in technology from your server, you must know the correct MIME content type for the plug-in and the file extensions you'll be using to store those files on your server. The producer of the plug-in will provide this information.

MIME types are managed through the IIS default Properties page. By clicking the File Types button from the Web server Properties panel, you can add, remove, and edit MIME types.

Necessary Procedures

Use the following procedure to add MIME types to your Web server:

1. Right-click on the local Web server and click Properties.

2. Click File Types.

3. Click New File Type.

4. Click New Type.

5. Enter the file extension for the MIME type.

6. Enter the MIME content type.

7. Click OK.

Exam Essentials

Understand the purpose of MIME types and how to manage them. MIME types inform Web browsers what plug-in to use to handle content sent from the server. You manage MIME types for your Web server in the default Properties page for the server.

Key Terms and Concepts

MIME type: A method of identifying the type of data in a content stream to browsers so the browser can select the proper tool to present the information. MIME types in IIS4 consist of file extensions related to MIME application types.

Sample Questions

1. You've installed a new streaming video delivery server on your Web server and installed a number of video files for your new Internet-based training service. All of your customers complain that they get an error message every time they click on the links that are supposed to start the video playback, even though they have the correct video plug-in installed. What must you do to fix this problem?

   A. Add the correct MIME type to the customers' browsers.

   B. Add the correct MIME type to your server.

   C. Reinstall the content server.

   D. Reinstall the customers' Web browsers.

   Answer: B. You must have a MIME type installed on your Web server that matches the extensions of the file you're serving so the server can identify the data type to the Web browser.

Manage the FTP service.

Chapter 2 covers management of FTP services in detail.

Critical Information

Refer to "Configure IIS to support the FTP service" in Chapter 2 for information about the management of FTP.

Necessary Procedures

Refer to "Configure IIS to support the FTP service" in Chapter 2 for FTP management procedures.

Exam Essentials

Refer to "Configure IIS to support the FTP service" in Chapter 2 for exam essentials relating to FTP service management.

Key Terms and Concepts

File Transfer Protocol (FTP): A TCP/IP-based client/server service which allows the upload and download of files to and from a server running the FTP service to a client running an FTP client. FTP is one of the oldest useful TCP/IP services, and is widely supported.

Sample Questions

1. You are co-locating an FTP server at your ISP's point-of-presence and will need to manage the FTP service remotely over the Internet from your office. Which solution is the most secure?

    A. Install Symantec's pcAnywhere remote control product, attach to the server whenever you need to manage it, and use the management tools on the remote server.

    B. Telnet to the server running Windows NT's built-in Telnet service and configure FTP by directly manipulating the metabase from the command prompt.

    C. Enter the server's TCP/IP address into your local MMC so the server appears, and simply use the MMC over the Internet.

    D. Use the HTML Internet Service Manager to connect to the server's admin Web site.

    Answer: D. A is highly non-secure, B would be difficult and non-secure even if NT came with a Telnet server (which it does not), and C requires leaving the full Workstation and Server services running on the remote machine, also highly non-secure.

Manage the WWW service.

Chapter 2 covers management of WWW services in detail.

Critical Information

Refer to "Configure IIS to support the WWW service" in Chapter 2 for information about the management of WWW services.

Necessary Procedures

Refer to "Configure IIS to support the WWW service" in Chapter 2 for WWW service management procedures.

Exam Essentials

Refer to "Configure IIS to support the WWW service" in Chapter 2 for exam essentials relating to WWW service management.

Key Terms and Concepts

World Wide Web (WWW):   A client/server file transfer and presentation protocol. Unlike FTP transfers, which are simply written to disk and stored when received, files transferred through the WWW service are opened by the receiving client (called a browser) and presented to the user by the method matching their MIME type. Common presentation types include text, hypertext, bitmapped graphics, sound, and video.

Sample Questions

1. You have created a Web site just for employees of your company and want to make sure that only authorized computers on your LAN can access the Web site. (You require this security precaution in addition to any other security precautions you have in place, such as firewalls or packet filters.) How can you enforce local-only access?

   A. Enable the Basic Authentication option in the Directory Security Properties tab.

   B. Add the network address and subnet mask of your network in the IP Address and Domain Name Restrictions exclusion list for the computer. Set the Web site to deny access by default.

   C. Require Secure Socket Layer connections to the Web site's home directory.

   D. Enable the Windows NT Challenge/Response option in the Directory Security Properties tab.

Answer: B. Without IP restrictions, an otherwise authorized user can access your network from outside your LAN (presuming that your LAN has a gateway to the Internet).

CHAPTER

4

Integration and Interoperability

Microsoft Exam Objectives Covered in This Chapter:

▶ **Configure IIS to connect to a database. Tasks
include:** *(pages 166 – 178)*

- Configuring ODBC

▶ **Configure IIS to integrate with Index Server. Tasks
include:** *(pages 178 – 188)*

- Specifying query parameters by creating the .idq file
- Specifying how the query results are formatted and displayed to
  the user by creating the .htx file

Thiss chapter covers two important aspects of the
exam: database connectivity and indexing. Both topics together
make up about 10% of the exam, so they're very important but not
as critical to your success on the exam as earlier chapters.

Configure IIS to connect to a database. Tasks include:

- Configuring ODBC

Databases power modern commerce. Any serious
attempt to use the Internet for direct commerce requires live
access to these databases and the information they store. IIS
supports attaching to databases through the Internet Database
Connector (IDC) and, more importantly, through Active Server
Pages (ASP).

IIS supports the ODBC (Open Database Connectivity) interface,
allowing nearly all database products to function interactively
over the Internet.

Windows NT 4 Option Pack comes with Data Access Components and Microsoft Transaction Server. Data Access Components is a suite of ActiveX objects and interfaces that allow the rapid development of Internet-enabled Web clients for databases. Transaction Server provides transaction support to ensure error- and corruption-free database exchanges over the Internet.

Critical Information

There are 5 basic steps to publishing a database on the Web with IIS:

1. Create the database using a traditional database product like MS SQL Server, Access, or FoxPro.

2. Create an ODBC interface to the database.

3. Configure IIS to support a dynamic database client Web site. This may include configuring Transaction Server to support atomic operations.

4. Create the Web site pages and scripts.

Step 1 is beyond the scope of this book—but we will go through a simple procedure to create and use an Access database for data storage.

The ODBC interface is the standard database interface that allows databases to access or link to other software products. ODBC provides a standard method to configure a database as a *data source*, or publisher of database information. Other software products (like IIS) can then link to those data sources to request (query) information from or store information to the database. Most database products that run under Windows support ODBC, so they can function as database engines for IIS. Figure 4.1 shows the Microsoft Access ODBC driver configured to host a database.

Because IIS controls the services that actually publish your database on the Internet, you will have to tell IIS how you want to deal with the data. You should create a folder to contain the site, create a virtual directory or virtual server to support it, and set the access permissions as appropriate. Remember that ASP scripts must have Execute permission assigned in IIS to function properly.

FIGURE 4.1: Microsoft Access ODBC driver configuration

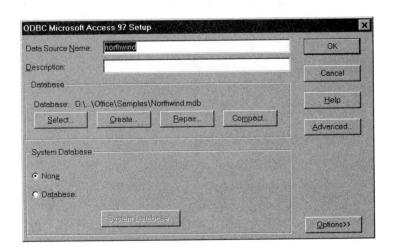

Creating site data using the Internet Database Connector

The IDC is an add-on to IIS that allows the dynamic publication of databases. Dynamic HTML databases are databases that are updated every time a Web browser requests them, so they contain up-to-the-minute snapshots of the database in question. This method of publication is different from simple static HTML databases, which are published manually whenever the database administrator gets around to it and do not contain changes more recent than the last publication.

IDC works as an extension to IIS, though it's actually an ISAPI application. When a browser requests a dynamic database, IIS reads the .idc file and performs the database connection and query instructions contained within it to create an HTML page. This HTML page contains the results of the database query stored in the .idc file and is formatted according to HTML format instructions contained in an associated .htx file. Since the database is required and a new HTML page is created each time a connection is made, data on the Web site is always in sync with data in the actual database.

TIP   Remember: The .idc file contains the query for retrieving the database information from the database server. The .htx file contains the instructions for formatting the data as HTML.

Some database products contain wizards to automatically create the .idc and .htx files required by the IDC. When you select the Dynamic HTML option in Microsoft's Publish to the Web Wizard in Access, you are creating the .idc and .htx files required by the IDC.

The IDC has no provisions for accepting database input from the Web, however—it is a one-way publication medium. You will have to use CGI scripts, ISAPI applications, or ASP if you want to update a database over the Internet. Figure 4.2 shows Microsoft Access's Publish to the Web Wizard creating a dynamic ASP-based database.

F I G U R E 4.2: Microsoft Access's Publish to the Web Wizard

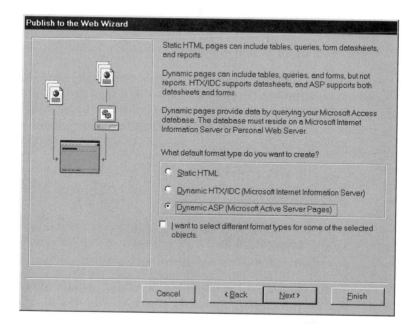

Dynamic HTML databases are convenient for their purpose, but they still don't allow remote users to add or edit the information they provide. ASP provides this functionality by running code on the Web server to extract information from the remote Web browser and push it into the ODBC-linked database driver running on the Web server. This ODBC driver may simply provide an interface to an existing SQL server, or it may start a database engine to store data into a database file. In either case, the software running on the Web server retrieves the existing client data and stores revised records into the database.

WARNING The directory containing your .asp files must have Execute permission set in the Internet Service Manager, or browsers will simply see your ASP code.

NOTE For more information on Active Server Pages, refer to *Mastering Internet Information Server 4* by Peter Dyson (Sybex, 1997).

Data Access Components

Windows NT 4 Option Pack comes with a set of related services, interfaces, and components called Microsoft Data Access Components (MDAC). These components are provided to ease the development of Internet-based client/server databases for larger databases such as SQL Server and Oracle. The core components of MDAC are:

Microsoft OLE DB, "middleware" that sits between the Web client and the server to translate standard OLE function calls into database-specific calls that a certain back-end database driver (for database engines SQL Server, Oracle, or Access) will understand. Essentially, OLE DB on the server lets you use the remaining components of MDAC to build your database application.

ActiveX Data Objects (ADO), a collection of ActiveX components that provide features to retrieve data from OLE DB–interfaced databases, manipulate that data, and return data to databases.

ADOs are pre-built and can be called from VBScripts as well as compiled Visual Basic and Visual C++ applications. These objects essentially allow you to rapidly develop ActiveX-based database applications without having to develop the ActiveX components yourself.

Remote Data Service (RDS), essentially a client-side data-caching service that allows clients to grab complete sets of data from a server, manipulate them locally, and return them to the server. This obviates network traffic that would be involved with interactive remote manipulation, thereby speeding the process and reducing network bandwidth requirements.

The online documentation covers these products in more detail for those who would like to build Internet database applications based on these technologies. You won't have to understand anything for the MCSE exam other than what the terms refer to. Unfortunately, the documentation that comes with these products is so jargon-filled and disjointed that unless you already understand ActiveX component-based development and three-tiered database development in detail you probably won't get anything useful out of it.

Microsoft Transaction Server

Microsoft Transaction Server is a middleware component that sits between the Internet-based client and the relational database back end. MTS is a set of programming interfaces to which your database clients must be written. The MTS application itself can be run on Windows NT, or on Windows 95 with DCOM support. If you fail to install DCOM support for Windows 95, installations under Windows 95 will fail. Additional information about MTS is available in the online documentation.

TIP Remember that MTS can be installed on Windows NT, or on Windows 95 with DCOM support.

Transaction Server provides the ability to create transactions, which are atomic (i.e., base-level indivisible) operations. The entire purpose of Transaction Server is to guarantee that one of two things will happen for every transaction:

- The transaction will succeed, and all components of the transaction will be correctly added to the database.

- The transaction will fail, and none of the components of the transaction will remain in the database.

This sounds simple, but it's critically important to the stability of a database system. Let's say that a banking transaction, such as a transfer between accounts, consists of two operations: a deduction from one account and an addition to another account. Because computers can actually do only one thing at a time, one of these operations occurs before the other. If the completion of the transaction is interrupted for any reason between the two portions of the transaction, the bank computer will be left with a deduction from one account with no corresponding addition to the other. Their database will be corrupt, and you, the client, will be out that much money until the bank figures out what went wrong.

Transaction Server prevents exactly this sort of problem. By packaging a set of functions into a single atomic transaction, you are telling MTS that either all of these functions must occur or none of them can occur—which doesn't really matter, because if they fail they can simply be retried later. Due to the normal delays encountered with Web-based database clients, the opportunity for failure during transactions increases dramatically, to the point that database systems would simply not be possible without the services of a transaction system like MTS.

Database Security

Databases frequently implement security on an object level (tables, queries, stored procedures, forms, and reports may have individual security permissions) to restrict the availability of data that the server will provide. Each database system implements security differently. Some (like MS SQL Server) are well integrated with the operating system and will automatically log you on to the database using your domain credentials. Others (like MS Access) are not built for a specific operating system and so must either log you on as an anonymous database user or ask for credentials when you open a secured database.

For Internet databases, the obvious problem is that users must be logged in correctly. For databases that are tightly integrated with the operating system, you must ensure that users coming in from the Web have properly authenticated with your server or they won't have the security permissions they expect. They'll get access-denied error messages because they're logged in as anonymous Internet users. Perhaps the easiest way to ensure proper authentication is to set security on the directory containing the Web pages that the users are initially greeted with. This will force their browsers either to authenticate behind the scenes (Windows NT Challenge/Response) or ask for credentials (Basic Authentication). Once a user is logged in properly, your database will behave as expected.

TIP The sorts of errors you'll encounter when Internet users are not logged in correctly vary widely depending upon the database product and the specific application in use. They often show up as either database login failures or object access errors.

Necessary Procedures

Use the following procedures to familiarize yourself with Web database publishing.

Configuring ODBC

1. Select Start ➤ Settings ➤ Control Panel.

2. Double-click the ODBC control panel.

3. Click the System DNS tab.

4. Click Add.

5. Double-click Microsoft Access Driver.

6. Type **northwind** in the Data Source Name input box.

7. Click Select.

8. Browse to `c:\program files\microsoft office\office\samples` or to the location of your Access sample files installation.

9. Select `northwind.mdb` and click OK.

10. Click OK.

11. Click OK to close the ODBC control panel.

Creating Site Files

1. Double-click My Computer and browse to `c:\inetpub\wwwroot\`.

2. Select File ➤ New ➤ Folder.

3. Type **northwind** and press Enter to rename the new folder.

4. Select Start ➤ Programs ➤ Microsoft Access to launch MS Access.

5. Click OK to open more files.

6. Browse to `c:\program files\microsoft office\office\samples` or the location of the Office or Access samples folder on your computer.

7. Double-click `northwind.mdb`.

8. Click OK to dismiss the opening dialog box.

9. Select File ➤ Save As HTML.

10. Click Next.

11. Click the All Objects tab.

12. Click Select All.

13. Click Next.

14. Click Browse.

15. Double-click `default.htm` and then click Next.

16. Click Dynamic ASP and then click Next.

17. Type **northwind** for the ODBC data source name.

18. Delete all the text in the server URL input line.

19. Click Next.

20. Click Browse.

21. Browse through the directory selector to `c:\inetpub\wwwroot\northwind`.

22. Click Select.

23. Click Next to publish locally.

24. Check Yes, I want to create a home page and then click Next.

25. Click Finish. The Access Web Publication wizard will create the site files to attach to your ODBC data source.

26. Close Microsoft Access.

Publishing data

1. Select Start ➤ Programs ➤ Windows NT 4 Option Pack ➤ Microsoft Internet Information Server ➤ Internet Service Manager.

2. Expand Internet Information Server and your computer name so that the Default Web Site is visible in the scope pane of the Management Console.

3. Right-click Default Web Site and Select New ➤ Virtual Directory.

4. Type **northwind** in the Alias input line.

5. Click Next.

6. Click Browse.

7. Browse to `c:\inetpub\wwwroot\northwind` or its equivalent on your system.

8. Click OK, then click Next. Enter a custom port (such as **8081**) or other unique identifier for this Web site.

9. Check the Execute permission in the Access control group.

10. Click Finish.

11. Select the northwind Web site and select Action ➤ Start.

You can now use your Web browser to test the Web site.

Exam Essentials

The following information is important to understand completely for the exam:

Know how to connect to a data source using ODBC. Set up ODBC data sources using the ODBC control panel.

Understand the purpose of Microsoft Transaction Server and its operating system compatibility. MTS allows discrete operations to be bound together into atomic units called transactions that either succeed or fail as a group. MTS runs under NT or under Windows 95 with DCOM support.

Understand how to deal with security and permissions issues in databases. Database permissions problems show up as object access denials and other related problems. Forcing a client browser logon on the Web pages that connect to the database will solve most security problems.

Key Terms and Concepts

Database: Stored sets of related information that can be retrieved using logical expressions (queries) that specify the set members desired.

Database client: A program that queries, displays, and updates database information. Also called a front end.

Database server: A program that stores databases and processes queries. Also called a back end.

Microsoft Transaction Server (MTS): A Microsoft product that provides the capability to bundle database operations as transactions.

Middleware: Software that performs protocol or data translation between the front end and the back end.

Open Database Connectivity (ODBC): A database middleware product that provides a translation between clients and servers so that any ODBC-capable client can connect to an ODBC-compatible server.

Transaction: A package of discrete events that in sum represent a single operation which must either succeed in entirety or fail in entirety. Transactions are used whenever partial success would cause data corruption.

Sample Questions

1. You've created an interactive database using Microsoft Access and Active Server Pages, but when you browse to the site, you get garbage on your screen that looks like a computer programming language rather than the database forms you expected. What's wrong?

   A. You haven't enabled Active Server Pages output in the IIS Manager.

   B. You selected the wrong type of output in the Publish to the Web Wizard in Microsoft Access.

   C. Your Web browser doesn't support Active Server Pages.

   D. You didn't set Execute permissions on the directory containing your database Web files.

   Answer: D. Active Server Pages requires Execute permissions.

2. You've set up an MS SQL Server application for workflow control and created a client based on ActiveX and Active Server Pages that runs over your company's intranet. While you developed the application on your own computer, you had no problems debugging the application. Users in the facility are also having no problems using the client through their Web browsers, but work-at-home users coming through the Internet receive an object access error message when they try to view database information. What is most likely wrong?

   A. SQL Server permissions are set incorrectly.

   B. IIS permissions are set incorrectly.

C. NTFS permissions are set incorrectly.

D. Remote users are logged in anonymously.

Answer: D. You must set security on an initial Web page to force the authentication of remote users.

3. You've set up an MS SQL Server application for workflow control and created a client based on ActiveX and Active Server Pages that runs over your company's intranet. After a few weeks of operation, users complain that some duplicate entries are appearing in certain databases. These duplicate entries are causing some customers to be overbilled. After debugging, you find that some work-at-home users are frustrated with the speed of their connection and click the Back button on their browsers to re-post information to the server when it's slow. This causes some records to be added to the database while other related records are interrupted. Which of the following solutions actually solves this problem?

A. Re-implement the application to use Transaction Server.

B. Increase the speed of your home users' Internet links.

C. Upgrade your server hardware so the application is more responsive.

D. Use Data Access Components to ensure data integrity.

Answer: A. This problem is caused because the process is interrupted, leaving garbage records behind. Speeding up the server doesn't actually solve the problem, it just decreases the likelihood of occurrence.

Configure IIS to integrate with Index Server. Tasks include:

- Specifying query parameters by creating the .idq file
- Specifying how the query results are formatted and displayed to the user by creating the .htx file

Critical Information

Interfacing queries to your Web pages can be as simple or as complex as you want to make it. To allow simple queries of your whole site, all you have to do is provide a link on your Web pages to a sample Web page that was installed when you installed the IIS software—link to /samples/search/query.htm on your own computer and you are done. This section shows you how to customize the way that Index Server queries your Web site.

Index Server, like ASP, is actually a set of Microsoft ISAPI applications. The Index Server DLL (IDQ.DLL) registers two file extensions for use with Index Server: .ida and .idq. Index Server also uses a third file type, .htx. To understand how Index Server works and to customize it for your site, you must know how these files interact. You should understand how the following components work:

- Query forms

- Internet Data Query (.idq) files

- HTML extension (.htx) files

- Internet Database Administration (.ida) files

Query Forms

Database queries start from query forms that look just like any other HTML form. Once you install Index Server on your Web site, you can embed the following form to any of your Web pages. The following form uses the sample search pages installed by Index Server in your Scripts directory.

```
<FORM ACTION="/scripts/samples/search/query.idq"
METHOD="POST">
Enter your query:
<INPUT TYPE="TEXT" NAME="CiRestriction" SIZE="60"
MAXLENGTH="100" VALUE=" ">
<INPUT TYPE="SUBMIT" VALUE="Execute Query">
<INPUT TYPE="RESET" VALUE="Clear">
```

```
<INPUT TYPE="HIDDEN" NAME="CiMaxRecordsPerPage"
VALUE="10">
<INPUT TYPE="HIDDEN" NAME="CiScope" VALUE="/">
<INPUT TYPE="HIDDEN" NAME="TemplateName" VALUE="query">
<INPUT TYPE="HIDDEN" NAME="CiSort" VALUE="rank[d]">
<INPUT TYPE="HIDDEN" NAME="HTMLQueryForm" VALUE="/
samples/search/query.htm">
</FORM>
```

This form has five hidden fields. The information in these five fields is passed on to the .idq file identified in the FORM ACTION field. You should also notice that query forms to the Index Server use the POST method.

This HTML text is not interpreted by IIS or by Index Server—the HTML form listed above instructs your Web browser to display the form to you. When you click the Execute Query button, the form data (the input fields with names, hidden or otherwise) are sent to the Web server with the request that the query.idq file be used to process it.

Internet Data Query (.idq) files

When IIS is asked to access an .idq file, it looks up the file extension in the registry and associates it with the IDQ.DLL ISAPI application. If that DLL is not already loaded into the IIS memory space, it is loaded now. Then control passes to IDQ.DLL, along with the location of the .idq file and the query data sent by the Web browser.

The IDQ.DLL application uses the .idq file to guide its processing of the query data. The .idq file contains parameters about the query such as the scope of the search, how many records (maximum) will be returned, how many will be returned in each query result page, what HTML template will be used, and how the results will be sorted.

Paths within the .idq files are from the virtual root of the server and cannot backtrack (i.e., they cannot access directories above the /wwwroot directory).

The .idq file consists of two sections:

Names defines nonstandard properties that this query may be limited on or display in the result. You can use this feature to index on special properties of documents that are indexed using content filters such as the content filter for Microsoft Office applications. This section is optional.

Query specifies the parameters of the query, such as the scope, columns, restrictions, and template. (These four parameters are required.) Parameters can (and some should) be passed from the HTML query form; for example, %Restriction% takes the restriction value—what you are searching for—from the field named Restriction in the HTML form.

Here is an example of an .idq file having the four required and two optional query parameters:

```
[QUERY]
CiRestriction=%CiRestriction%
CiColumns=filename,size,characterization,vpath,DocTitle
,write
CiScope=%CiScope%
CiFlags=DEEP
CiTemplate=/scripts/result.htx
CiSort=%CiSort%
```

To use the preceding .idq file, you must place the result.htx file in the /scripts subdirectory, of course. You can use the .idq files to create multiple catalogs simply by creating multiple .idq files, each with a separate CiCatalog setting. For example, if one .idc had the settings:

```
CiCatalog=C:\Inetpub\Catalog1\
CiScope=\firstroot
```

and another .idc was identical except for the settings:

```
CiCatalog=C:\Inetpub\Catalog2\
CiScope=\secondroot
```

then you would have two catalogs: one in the `Catalog1` subdirectory, which allows the user to find files from the `\firstroot` subdirectory, and the other in the `Catalog2` subdirectory, which allows the user to find files from the `\secondroot` subdirectory. Note, however, that the preceding example doesn't keep both catalogs from indexing your entire Web site. It just establishes two directories and allows both to be searched with a restriction on each.

A better use for the CiScope parameter is to limit queries to certain parts of your Web site when the network user is looking for particular information. For example, if you have separate subdirectories for new products, current products, press releases, device drivers, and technical documentation, then you can create specialized `.idq` files for each area of your Web site. That way, browsers of your Web site won't have to wade through extraneous information that just happens to match the search criteria the user types in. This technique is used in Internet search engines that allow you to select whether the search is conducted on the whole site or only on focused sections.

HTML Extension (.htx) Files

IDQ.DLL uses the parameters from the `.idq` page to search its database. It needs another file to tell it how to format the resulting data so that IIS can send it to the Web browser, and `.htx` files are Microsoft's answer to that problem.

The `.htx` documents are almost like programming languages because they must be able to respond to various conditions; for example, no files match your query, one page worth of files match, or many HTML pages worth of files match. Other than the special conditional constructs (e.g., the `%if` statement and `%endif` statement) and the commands to insert data returned from the query (e.g., `%filename%` and `%DocTitle%`), the `.htx` document contains regular HTML-formatted text.

The following `.htx` file is very simple; it is merely an example of how an `.htx` file is formatted. You should use the more complicated query sample files installed with Index Server—or edit them to suit the needs of your Web site.

```
<HTML>
<!--
  <%CiTemplate%>
-->
<HEAD>
<TITLE>SEARCH</TITLE>
</HEAD>
<%begindetail%>
  <p>
  <dt>
    <%CiCurrentRecordNumber%>.
    <%if DocTitle isempty%>
      <b><a href="<%EscapeURL vpath%>"><%filename%></
a></b>
    <%else%>
      <b><a href="<%EscapeURL vpath%>"><%DocTitle%></
a></b>
    <%endif%>
  <dd>
    <b><i>Abstract: </i></b><%characterization%>
    <br>
    <cite>
      <a href="<%EscapeURL vpath%>">http://
<%server_name%><%vpath%></a>
      <font size=-1> - <%if size eq ""%>(size and time
unknown)<%else%>size <%size%> bytes - <%write%>
GMT<%endif%></font>
    </cite>
<%enddetail%>
</HTML>
```

Internet Database Administration (.ida) Files

One more type of file that you should be familiar with to customize
Index Server for your Web site is the .ida file type. These files are like
.idq files except that .ida files are focused on the overall housekeeping

of the Index Server, instead of the actual queries. Furthermore, .ida files accept only four parameters:

CiCatalog specifies where the catalog is located. If it is missing, the default location specified in the registry is used.

CiTemplate specifies the template file (i.e., .htx or .htm file) that will be used to format the data that results from execution of the .ida command.

CiAdministration specifies use of the administrative command, which must be one of the following: UpdateDirectories, GetState, ForceMerge, or ScanDirectories. If nothing is specified, the administrative action will default to GetState.

CiLocale specifies locale information such as the character set or time zone in use.

The administration .ida file for updating the virtual directories that is installed when you install Index Server is as follows:

```
[Admin]
CiCatalog=C:\Inetpub\
CiTemplate=/srchadm/admin.htm
CiAdminOperation=UpdateDirectories
```

The administration .ida file for forcing a master merge that is installed when you install Index Server is as follows:

```
[Admin]
CiCatalog=C:\Inetpub\
CiTemplate=/srchadm/admin.htm
CiAdminOperation=ForceMerge
```

The administration .ida file for forcing a scan of the virtual directories that is installed when you install Index Server is as follows:

```
[Admin]
CiCatalog=C:\Inetpub\
CiTemplate=/srchadm/admin.htm
CiAdminOperation=ScanDirectories
```

The administration .ida file for getting statistics on Index Server that is installed when you install Index Server is as follows:

```
[Admin]
CiCatalog=C:\Inetpub\
CiTemplate=/Scripts/srchadm/state.htx
CiAdminOperation=GetState
```

These four administrative files don't seem like much for the results they produce. Most of the work is actually done in the IDQ.DLL program, and the results are formatted using the admin.htm and state.htx files. You should have no reason to modify the admin.htm and the state .htx files, but you may want to modify the .ida files to customize the functionality of Index Server for your site.

For example, you might want to create .ida files that allow you to manage separate master catalogs. You could create two sets of .ida files, like those shown in the example, except that the CiCatalog entry for one would point to the C:\InetPub\Catalog1 and the other set would point to C:\InetPub\Catalog2. You could then use these administration pages (using the UpdateDirectories .ida command) to limit the virtual directories that each will index. You will end up with two (or more) catalogs that index different portions of your Web site. You can then use specialized .idq files (as described in the section on Internet Data Query files) to search these limited catalogs.

Necessary Procedures

The following two procedures show you how to access two query-related files provided in one of the default sample files that comes with IIS. You must have installed IIS samples when you installed IIS for these procedures to work.

Specifying query parameters by creating the .idq file

1. Select Start ➢ Programs ➢ Accessories ➢ Notepad.

2. Select File ➢ Open.

3. Browse to c:\inetpub\iissamples\exair\search or the location of the ExAir sample site on your computer.

4. Select All files in the Files of Type pick box.

5. Double-click query.idq in the files list box.

6. Read through the file in detail. In addition to showing actual IDQ variables, this document explains the purpose of each variable in detail.

7. Close Notepad.

Specifying how the query results are formatted and displayed to the user by creating the .htx file

1. Select Start ➢ Programs ➢ Accessories ➢ Notepad.

2. Select File ➢ Open.

3. Browse to c:\inetpub\iissamples\exair\search or the location of the ExAir sample site on your computer.

4. Select All files in the Files of Type pick box.

5. Double-click query.htx in the files list box.

6. Read through the file in detail. In addition to showing actual HTX variables, this document explains the purpose of each variable in detail.

7. Close Notepad.

Exam Essentials

The following information is critical to your success on the exam:

Understand the purpose of the various Index Server–related files.   IDQ files specify the scope and restrictions of a search. HTX files provide a template Web page for the formatting of query results. The IDA file is used to control administrative functions for the indexed site.

Know how to limit the scope of a query. Queries are limited to Web sites and the directories in that Web site. Further scope restrictions are performed by editing the IDQ file for the Web site.

Key Terms & Concepts

HTML extension (.htx) files: Files used by the IDQ.DLL to format the returned data from a query as HTML files.

Internet Database Administration (.ida) files: Files loaded by the IDQ.DLL to specify global administrative parameters.

Internet Data Query (.idq) files: Files used by the IDQ.DLL to specify the scope and restrictions of a query.

Sample Questions

1. You want to limit the scope of queries from within the /Products/ Software/Downloads section of your Web site to just that section of your Web site. You want to be able to query your whole site from the home page, however. How can you do this most easily?

   A. Set the CiScope value in the .idq file to /Products/Software/ Downloads.

   B. Remove Read permission for the IUSR_SEARCH user from all directories except for the /Products/Software/Downloads directory.

   C. Disable indexing on all virtual directories except for the /Products/Software/Downloads virtual directory.

   D. You cannot limit the scope of a query.

   Answer: A. The CiScope value limits the scope of the query.

2. You have an Active Server Pages program that interacts with an ActiveX control to accept query parameters and feed them to the Internet Database Connector for a bibliography search of technical papers authored by professors at your university. The search process works great but you would like to liven up the format of the resulting output Web pages by adding some graphics and links back to your home page. Which file should you modify?

A. Query.asp

B. IDC.DLL

C. Bibform.htx

D. Query.idc

Answer: C. The .htx file specifies the format of the data resulting from the query. The .idc file specifies how the query should be presented to the database. The .asp file presents the original query form that the user enters search terms into. The .DLL is the executable extension to IIS that performs the queries as specified by the .idc and .htx files.

CHAPTER

5

Running Applications

Microsoft Exam Objectives Covered in This Chapter:

▶ **Configure IIS to support server-side scripting.** *(pages 191 – 195)*

▶ **Configure IIS to run ISAPI applications.** *(pages 195 – 204)*

Internet Information Server by itself is a fast and secure platform for serving HTML files to Web browsers. Internet Server Application Programming Interface (ISAPI) and Active Server Pages (ASP) give IIS additional flexibility and power by generating Web pages dynamically when the Web pages are needed.

Dynamic Web pages can be activated a number of ways, including directly from the Address field of a Web browser, from a hypertext link, and from a form. ISAPI applications can run in the same address space as IIS or in a separate memory space and therefore can be faster than other dynamic content methods like the Common Gateway Interface (CGI) used by most other Web server operating systems (CGI is also supported by IIS).

ISAPI applications are written to a specialized interface in a compiled programming language such as C++. ISAPI applications can perform complex operations on their own or they can be interpreters for scripting languages such as Perl, TCL, Visual Basic, or JScript. ISAPI can also be used to implement filters, which extend the functionality of IIS and can affect how all communications stream in and out of IIS.

Active Server Pages uses an ISAPI Dynamic Link Library (DLL) as a scripting host to implement the VBScript and JScript scripting languages on the server side. These scripts are used to create HTML files before the HTML is sent to the browser. VBScript and JScript are the same language modules used on the client side in Web browsers, although there are some inherent differences between the server and client environments.

Configure IIS to support server-side scripting.

Server-side scripting is the use of scripting languages like Visual Basic or JScript to dynamically create Web pages on demand in the Web server. Also called Active Server Pages, server-side scripting is implemented by the ASP.DLL ISAPI application, which acts as a filter on the output stream to convert .asp files into HTML as they're transmitted to the user.

Critical Information

There isn't anything special you have to do to support server-side scripting, since IIS is configured to support it by default. All you actually need to do is hyperlink .asp files to your Web site. Web sites or virtual directories that contain ASP files must have the Script or Execute permissions set in the Home Directory tab of the Web site's Properties panel. Figure 5.1 shows the Web site Properties panel configured for ASP.

ASPs are HTML pages that contain scripts written in VBScript or JScript, as well as regular HTML text. ASPs have the extension .asp, which is listed in the extensions that are associated with CGI and ISAPI applications. The .asp extension is associated with the ASP.DLL ISAPI application. When a Web browser requests a page with an .asp extension, IIS sends the .asp file to ASP.DLL for processing before transmitting it to the user.

NOTE Windows NT will only prompt for authentication if you disable anonymous login and secure your Web site files against access by the IUSR_*computername* account.

F I G U R E 5.1: Scripting is enabled for this Web site

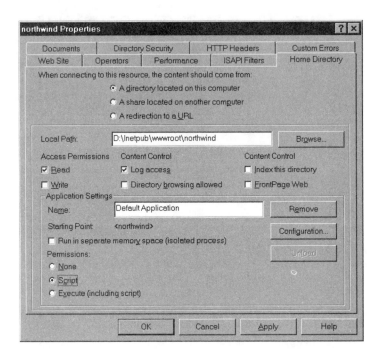

When IIS is asked to return a file ending in `.asp`, it recognizes that the ASP ISAPI filter must first process the file. The ASP filter processes the `.asp` file sequentially until it encounters a scripting language portion of the `.asp` page. (The special symbols <% and %> surround the scripting language portions of the `.asp` document.)

ASP.DLL interprets the scripting language portion(s) of the document using the default scripting language for the page, which is VBScript unless the DefaultScriptLanguage registry key is changed or a command such as <%@ LANGUAGE=JScript %> appears at the beginning of the document. The results of the scripted action must either be in HTML code to be viewed on the client browser or be understood by a registered MIME type.

You can also include scripts in `.asp` files using the SCRIPT LANGUAGE and RUNAT HTML tags. For example, <SCRIPT LANGUAGE=JScript RUNAT=Server> identifies the start of a JScript code segment that will run on the server. A script code segment defined in this manner ends with the </SCRIPT> HTML tag.

SEE ALSO   Just as it is not the purpose of this book to teach you HTML, it is not the purpose of this book to teach you JScript and VBScript programming. You should refer to other books, such as *Web Pages that Suck* (Sybex, 1998), for information on Web and HTML design, and to Microsoft's documentation for information on how to develop useful ASP programs. Check out Sybex's Web site at www.sybex.com for a full range of Web development book titles.

You can use ASP scripts to do many of the HTML text generation functions that you can do with CGI executables and ISAPI applications. The primary advantage of ASP scripts, however, is that you can embed them right in with regular HTML text and develop them quickly.

Necessary Procedures

Use the following procedure to modify scripting permissions for a Web site:

1. Start the MMC.

2. Expand the scope pane to display the default Web site.

3. Right-click on the default Web site and select Properties.

4. Select the Home Directory tab.

5. Select the Execute (including Script) permission.

6. Click Apply.

7. Click Select All.

8. Click OK.

9. Click OK.

10. Close the MMC.

Exam Essentials

Understand how ASP scripts are implemented by IIS. ASP is an ISAPI filter DLL that interprets Visual Basic and JScript commands embedded in HTML documents to create resulting HTML that is returned to the Web browser.

Understand the security requirements to execute ASP scripts. The IIS Script or Execute permissions must be set on the Web site or virtual directory containing ASP scripts in order for them to be executed. Otherwise, the ASP scripting code will be returned to the user.

Key Terms and Concepts

Active Server Pages: A server-side dynamic content technology that implements a scripting host like Visual Basic or JScript as an ISAPI filter DLL.

JScript: The Microsoft variant of JavaScript, a simple scripting language developed by Netscape based on the syntax of Sun's Java programming language.

Visual Basic: A simple scripting language included in most Microsoft applications and operating systems. VBScript is the variant used by the Windows Scripting Host, Internet Explorer, and Internet Information Server.

Sample Questions

1. You have embedded a small routine to count the number of times a page has been accessed (using <% and %> to enclose the JScript program) in the file summary.html. Rather than executing the program, however, IIS just returns the program as you typed it in the resulting Web page. You verify that the directory has Script access enabled. What is wrong?

   A. You must remove the Read access for the directory.

B. You must enable Execute (including Script) access for the directory.

C. You must install a JScript interpreter ISAPI DLL.

D. You must rename the file to have an `.asp` extension.

Answer: D. IIS will only scan the HTML page for scripts to execute if it has an extension, such as `.asp`, associated with a scripting DLL, such as ASP.DLL.

2. Your company will be creating a Human Resources site for internal use so employees can check their accrued vacation hours and other benefits. You want to provide a customized Web page for each employee that is generated when they access the site. Which solution will take the least effort to implement simple animation?

A. Develop a WIN-CGI executable.

B. Develop an ISAPI application.

C. Develop an ASP script.

D. Develop an ISAPI filter.

Answer: C. ASP provides the fastest and most customizable method for returning custom content.

Configure IIS to run ISAPI applications.

ISAPI provides a way for programmers to extend the functionality of IIS. There are two means to do this:

- **ISAPI applications,** which execute when a page with a specific extension is requested by a browser, and which parse the data on that page to return output to the requesting browser. ISAPI applications could be used to implement a scripting language like Visual Basic or Perl.

- **ISAPI filters,** which process all information returned by a Web site. ISAPI filters can be used to implement encryption or translation functions that must be performed on every page returned by a Web site.

Critical Information

ISAPI applications are DLLs that are activated when the WWW service is asked to return a page whose file extension is recorded in the registry as an ISAPI file type. If the recorded entry points to an executable program (i.e., a program that ends in .exe and has %s %s parameters), then IIS starts that program as a CGI executable. If the recorded entry points to a file that ends in .dll, then ISAPI loads the dynamic link library into its own memory space and passes control to it.

Figure 5.2 shows the default ISAPI DLL to extension mappings for ISAPI applications that come with Internet Information Server.

FIGURE 5.2: Default ISAPI DLL extension mappings

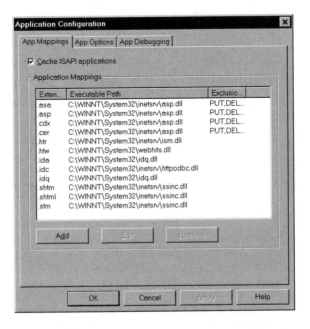

In IIS3, ISAPI DLLs ran in the same memory space as IIS. In IIS4, you can separate each ISAPI DLL into its own memory space. This increases fault tolerance and security, because now a DLL that crashes won't bring down IIS and possibly your server as well. Furthermore, a security violation inside the memory space of a DLL won't provide access to the IIS memory space. Figure 5.3 shows the sample Exploration Air virtual directory configured to run in its own memory space.

F I G U R E 5.3: A Web application configured to run in its own memory space

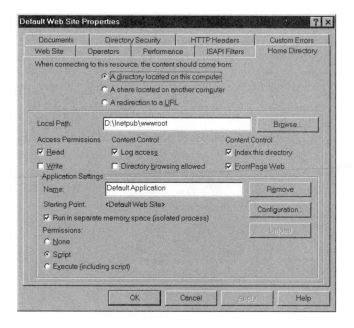

ISAPI DLLs are usually quite a bit faster than CGI executables because they're optimized to work with IIS. Also, ISAPI DLLs do not have to be loaded and run each time a Web page using them is accessed, because the IIS ISAPI mechanism can use the same copy of the DLL in memory for each access. This arrangement reduces the data transfer time between IIS and the ISAPI DLL and allows the

DLL to respond faster than a CGI executable that performs the same function. ISAPI DLLs are more difficult to write, however, because they require a specialized programming environment (most commonly Microsoft C++ with the Win32 SDK, although some people have had success using other compiler environments).

An ISAPI application can do anything that a CGI executable can do, including running scripts. Many scripting languages have been implemented as ISAPI DLLs; one example is Perl, which is currently the most popular server-side scripting language for developing Web pages. (However, JScript and VBScript, which are also implemented by Microsoft as ISAPI DLLs, may soon eclipse Perl.)

After you configure IIS to activate the ISAPI DLL when a file with its extension is accessed, you can treat the ISAPI application just like a CGI executable. You interface to an ISAPI application (i.e., pass parameters to it) the same way you interface to a CGI executable (via a URL, from a hypertext link, or from a HTML form).

ISAPI DLLs extend the functionality of the WWW service of IIS. ISAPI DLLs respect the same NTFS restrictions as IIS. For example, if a user is logged on anonymously, the ISAPI DLL will be able to access only resources available to the IUSR_*computername* account. If the user has attached to the WWW service using the Administrator account, then the ISAPI DLL will be able to access any resources that the Administrator account can access.

TIP Study the NTFS permission environment for ISAPI DLLs carefully.

Because an ISAPI program may access more than the WWW service will normally permit (i.e., it can access directories that are not in the list of home or virtual directories for the WWW service), you must be careful to construct ISAPI programs that access only the data you want accessed. Or you should make sure that the users with permission to run the ISAPI program (including the IUSR_*computername* anonymous user account) have NTFS permissions to access only the files and directories that you determine are safe.

The user of an ISAPI application must have Execute permission for the directory containing the application (.dll) program. The user doesn't need Read access to that directory unless the DLL itself has some reason to read a file in that directory. If the ISAPI application is a script interpreter, however, the user must have NTFS Read permission to the directory containing the script.

Filters extend the functionality of IIS directly by modifying the output of the Web server as it is passed to the browser. Configuring IIS to use an ISAPI filter is a simple matter of installing the filter in a directory with appropriate permissions and using the Internet Service Manager to bind that filter to either the Web server for global filters or to a specific Web site. Using the ISAPI filter, however, requires that you know what the filter does and how it is used. There is no standard as to what filters may do to your IIS server. The whole point of filters is to extend the capabilities of IIS in new and unexpected (to Microsoft programmers, at least) ways. Figure 5.4 shows the default filters set up to process all data served by IIS.

FIGURE 5.4: Default global IIS filters

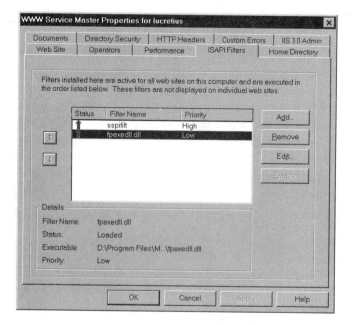

The other use for ISAPI DLLs is to directly extend the functionality of the WWW service of IIS. ISAPI DLLs can be written to preprocess the HTTP requests and to postprocess the HTTP responses of IIS. You can use filters for the following purposes:

- authentication (for other than Windows NT security)

- specialized encryption or compression

- more elaborate access restrictions (such as by Internet name as well as by IP address)

- implementation of HTTP commands that IIS does not yet support

- additional specialized server-side include commands that execute faster because they do not require file access

- additional logging and traffic analyses beyond what the built-in logging features provide

When you develop an ISAPI filter, you register which server actions the filter will respond to. It can, for example, preprocess the raw data sent from the client, the headers sent by the client, the data that will be sent to a CGI executable or ISAPI application, the data returned by an application, and final data that will be sent to the Web browser.

To configure an ISAPI filter to work on all Web traffic, install the filter on the WWW Master Properties ISAPI Filters tab.

A correctly written filter will, when initialized by IIS, register which WWW service events it will process. You can apply a filter globally to all IIS-supported services by adding it to IIS, or you can apply a filter to certain Web sites. When you add a global filter, you must stop and start IIS to apply the filter. When you add a filter to a Web site, it will automatically load when a page from that Web site is requested for the first time.

Necessary Procedures

Configuring IIS to pass control to a specific ISAPI DLL based on the requested file's extension is easy:

1. Launch the MMC and right-click on the Web site or virtual directory you want the ISAPI application associated with.

2. Select Properties, and select the Directory tab.

3. Click the Configuration button in the Application Settings control group.

4. Click Add to add the ISAPI DLL executable and the extensions to which it should respond.

The following process shows you how to add filters to specific Web sites:

1. Select the ISAPI Filters tab of the Web site's Properties panel.

2. Click Add.

3. Enter a descriptive name for the filter in the Filter Name input box.

4. Enter the path to the Dynamic Link Library.

5. Click the up or down arrows to increase or decrease the filter's execution priority relative to its peer filters. Filters modify the data stream from top to bottom in the order shown on the ISAPI Filters tab.

Exam Essentials

Understand the purpose of ISAPI applications and how to add them to Web sites.   ISAPI applications allow you to extend IIS to perform very specific processing based on a file's extension before the file is returned to a Web browser. They are added to Web sites and virtual directories through the Home Directory tab of the Properties panel.

Understand the purpose of ISAPI filters and how to add them to Web sites. ISAPI filters are used to process all communications between a Web server and browser. They are added to all Web sites through the Master Properties control panel or to a specific Web site through the ISAPI Filters tab of the Web site's Properties panel.

Key Terms and Concepts

Dynamic Link Library (DLL): Separate code modules that can be independently loaded and executed to extend the functionality of a program.

Filter: A specific ISAPI DLL that is inserted into the communications stream to process all information transmitted by a Web site or server.

Internet Service Applications Programming Interface (ISAPI): A Microsoft specification for creating IIS-compatible Web server extensions.

Sample Questions

1. You wish to efficiently extend IIS to support encrypted communications for all Web pages using the BLOWFISH cipher. Which environment best fits your needs?

   A. JScript

   B. An ISAPI application

   C. CGI

   D. An ISAPI filter

   Answer: D. An ISAPI filter is an excellent way to control or extend how IIS handles its communications.

2. Your company has recently licensed language translation software that can automatically translate your Web site into any one of six different major languages. Your Web site changes rapidly, so static

translation is not a viable option. You need to apply this function to all the Web pages on your site automatically. The vendor is providing source code that your development team can customize as necessary. Which application format is most appropriate for this function?

A. A WIN-CGI executable

B. An ISAPI application

C. An ASP script

D. An ISAPI filter

Answer: D. Filters are used whenever a specific function should be applied to all the documents coming from a server or Web site.

3. How do you configure a Web site to use an ISAPI DLL?

A. In the Home Directory tab of the Web site click Configuration and add an extension and a path to the file in the App Mappings tab.

B. In the HTTP Headers tab of the Web site click Configuration and add an extension and a path to the file in the App Mappings tab.

C. With the Registry Editor add an extension and a path to the file in the ScriptMap registry key.

D. With the Registry Editor add an extension and a path to the file in the MimeMap registry key.

Answer: A. With IIS4 you no longer have to edit the registry to add an ISAPI DLL to a Web site.

4. You have an ISAPI DLL that provides encrypted communications to your Web site using the Triple DES cipher. You want that DLL to run in a separate memory space from other DLLs for security reasons and so you can start and stop that DLL separately from other IIS applications. How can you most easily achieve your objective?

A. Re-implement the DLL as a CGI script.

B. Run multiple copies of IIS.

    C. Start IIS from the Run... item in the Start menu. Check the Run in Separate Memory Space option.

    D. Check the Run in Separate Memory Space option in the Home Directory tab of the Web site.

Answer: D. You can cause the ISAPI DLLs for a directory to run in a separate memory space by clicking the option in that directory's tab.

CHAPTER

6

Monitoring and Optimization

Microsoft Exam Objectives Covered in This Chapter:

▶ **Maintain a log for fine-tuning and auditing purposes. Tasks include:** *(pages 207 – 216)*
- Importing log files into a Usage Import and Report Writer database
- Configuring the logging features of the WWW service
- Configuring the logging features of the FTP service
- Configuring Usage Import and Report Writer to analyze logs created by the WWW service or the FTP service
- Automating the use of Usage Import and Report Writer

▶ **Monitor performance of various functions by using Performance Monitor. Functions include HTTP and FTP sessions.** *(pages 217 – 222)*

▶ **Analyze performance. Performance issues include:** *(pages 222 – 225)*
- Identifying bottlenecks
- Identifying network-related performance issues
- Identifying disk-related performance issues
- Identifying CPU-related performance issues

▶ **Optimize performance of IIS.** *(pages 226 – 230)*

▶ **Optimize performance of Index Server.** *(pages 231 – 237)*

▶ **Optimize performance of Microsoft SMTP Service.** *(pages 237 – 240)*

▶ **Optimize performance of Microsoft NNTP Service.** *(pages 240 – 242)*

▶ **Interpret performance data.** *(pages 242 – 243)*

▶ **Optimize a Web site by using Content Analyzer.** *(pages 243 – 249)*

Maintain a log for fine-tuning and auditing purposes. Tasks include:

- Importing log files into a Usage Import and Report Writer database
- Configuring the logging features of the WWW service
- Configuring the logging features of the FTP service
- Configuring Usage Import and Report Writer to analyze logs created by the WWW service or the FTP service
- Automating the use of Usage Import and Report Writer

Critical Information

The logs created by IIS are a gold mine of information on how your server is used. They are also useful for figuring out how well your server performs over time and what parts of your Web site(s) are the most popular and therefore are consuming the most bandwidth to your server.

Unfortunately, these logs create an enormous amount of information. You can log to an ODBC data source like a Microsoft Access database or an SQL Server, query the data, and then create reports to view any statistics you want, but that process takes a lot of setup effort. IIS provides a separate product called Report Writer that can perform much of this work for you.

Report Writer is the part of Site Server Express that takes the log data stored by IIS and helps you understand how your site is being accessed. With Report Writer (and Usage Import) you can easily separate out important information from the voluminous amount of data a busy

Web site can generate. You can track such data as the most frequently accessed pages, the most common errors, the times of greatest site access, and even where most of your accesses come from.

The first thing you have to do when working with IIS log data is to get the data you want into the log file you want. You do this through the logging settings of each Web and FTP site, or you can set the default logging characteristics for all of the Web sites and FTP sites in IIS.

Settings you can configure include the type of log file created, which may be:

- Microsoft IIS Log File Format
- NCSA Common Log File Format
- ODBC Logging
- W3C Extended Log File Format

The W3C Extended Log File Format is the default setting and it is also the most flexible format because it allows you to select what goes into the data files.

The more data you put in your log file, the larger and faster your log files will grow. For lightly loaded Web servers, however, the more information you have to work with the better.

Before you can work with the log data, you have to import it into Report Writer. You do this through the Usage Import tool shown in Figure 6.1. The Usage Import tool can be found alongside the rest of the Site Server Express tools, in Start ➢ Programs ➢ Windows NT 4.0 Option Pack ➢ Site Server 2.0 Express ➢ Usage Import.

The Usage Import tool has to be configured to retrieve data generated by your Web site. When you first start it up it will ask for the log file format, domain name, and home page location for the Web site. You then may specify the location of the log files to import.

By default, the log files are stored in the LogFiles subdirectory of your Windows NT System32 directory. Each Web site (and FTP site) gets its own subdirectory of LogFiles. The default Web site stores its log files in the W3SVC1 subdirectory.

FIGURE 6.1: You use the Usage Import tool to transform the IIS log files into a format that Report Writer can use

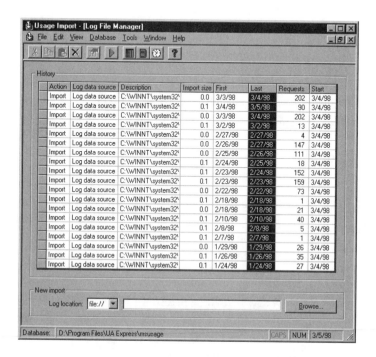

The W3SVC1 subdirectory (or whichever subdirectory you are using) may contain many log files, depending on how you have set up logging for your Web site. The default setting is to create a new log file every day. When selecting a log file to import, you can select more than one.

The data, when imported, ends up in an .mdb file. This is the same format of database file used by Microsoft Access, so you can use your regular database tools to manipulate it. If you want to generate common Web reports from it, you can use the Report Writer program, described in the next section.

Several reports in the Report Writer tool require more data than is actually stored in the IIS log files. The log files, for example, store IP addresses but not the Internet names of the computers attaching to the Web server. If you want to know the names of the computers connecting to your server, you have to query the DNS server to match the numbers to their names. Usage Import will do this for you, as well as do Whois queries (in order to determine information about the organization responsible for the computer) and title lookup (which connects to each URL referenced in the log file and extracts the title of the HTML page).

These operations can take a great deal of time (up to several seconds for each entry!) and take up significant amounts of Internet bandwidth that could otherwise be used by clients attaching to your Web site, so you should only perform these operations if you really want the reports that are based on them.

One of the nice features of Usage Import (there are too many features to list here) is that you can make data imports happen automatically. If you have a new log file being generated every night at midnight, for example, you might configure Usage Import to import the just-finished log. You use the Scheduler tool to create and schedule the import.

The Scheduler (which you will also use in Report Writer) organizes its activities into Jobs and Tasks. You schedule a job to happen at a specific time, and that job may consist of several tasks, including importing data from the log files.

Once you have the data imported into the .mdb database, you can generate reports using Report Writer (see Figure 6.2.). If you try to use Report Writer before importing the data, you will end up with some nice-looking but otherwise useless reports. Report Writer has a number of predefined reports you can choose from, divided into detail reports and summary reports.

The extra data in the log files really doesn't take up a lot more space, and doesn't slow down IIS significantly, but performing IP resolution, Whois queries, and title lookup operations can slow down the reporting process considerably for a WWW site with a lot of log data requirements. Consider performing those operations and running those reports less frequently than regular reports, and do it

FIGURE 6.2: Report Writer has many forms that make the data generated by IIS's logging feature easier to understand

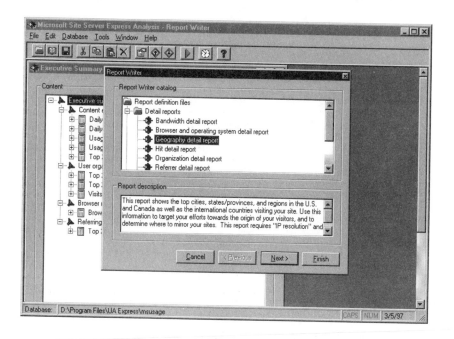

when bandwidth on the Internet is not at a premium (you could, for example, configure Usage Import to perform such operations at five in the morning on Sundays).

With data from reports, such as the Request detail report, that show the most-accessed pages, you can spend your time optimizing those pages. For instance, the most frequently accessed file on your site might be a logo graphic that occurs in many different Web pages. By reducing the size of that single file and converting it to a monochrome image, you could dramatically reduce the load on your server.

Necessary Procedures

Configure the Logging Features of the WWW and FTP Services

This procedure guides you through the process of customizing the data reported by the default FTP and Web sites.

1. Start the Microsoft Management Console.

2. Right-click the default FTP site for your computer and select Properties.

3. Click the FTP Site tab.

4. Make sure the Enable Logging button is selected.

5. Click the Properties button.

6. Click the Extended Properties tab.

7. Click the Date, User Name, Bytes Sent, Bytes Received, and Time Taken options.

8. Click Apply, then click OK. Click OK again.

9. Right-click the Default Web site for your computer and select Properties.

10. Click the Web Site tab.

11. Make sure the Enable Logging button is selected.

12. Click the Properties button.

13. Click the Extended Properties tab.

14. Click the Date, User Name, Bytes Sent, Bytes Received, and Protocol Version options.

15. Click Apply, then click OK. Click OK again.

Import Log Files into a Usage Import and Report Writer Database

Use the following procedure to import log files into a Usage Import and Report Writer database:

1. Click around the sample site a bit using your Web browser (enter http://localhost/ in the address field) in order to generate some data to import.

2. Start Usage Import by selecting Start ➢ Programs ➢ Windows NT 4.0 Option Pack ➢ Site Server 2.0 Express ➢ Usage Import.

3. Click OK to the message that there are no Internet sites configured.

4. Click OK to accept Microsoft IIS W3C Extended Log File Format.

5. Enter the domain name of your computer in the Local Domain field and press OK.

6. Enter http://*host_name/* in the Home Page URLs field and click OK.

7. At the end of the Log Location field in the middle of the screen click the Browse... button.

8. Go to the location where your log files are stored on the computer (usually winnt\system32\logfiles on the drive where the operating system files are stored).

9. Select the W3SVC1 folder.

10. Select all of the files in the directory (click the first file in the directory then hold down the Shift key on the keyboard and click the last file in the directory).

11. Click the Open button.

12. Select File ➢ Start Import or click the green triangle on the button bar.

13. Click the OK button. Click the Close button.

14. Close Usage Import.

Automate the Use of Usage Import and Report Writer

Use this procedure to automate the use of Usage Import and Report Writer:

1. Start Usage Import by selecting Start ➤ Programs ➤ Windows NT 4.0 Option Pack ➤ Site Server 2.0 Express ➤ Usage Import.

2. Select Tools ➤ Scheduler.

3. Right-click the All Jobs item and select New Job.

4. Check the Active box.

5. Select Every Wednesday at 12:00 A.M.

6. Click OK.

7. Right-click the New Job item and select New Task.

8. Select Import Log File as the Task type.

9. Enter **w3c** in the Log Data Source.

10. Enter the path to your log files in the Log Location field (replace the date with $1. For example, you might enter **c:\winnt\ system32\logfiles\w3svc1\ex$1.log**).

11. Click OK.

Configure Usage Import and Report Writer to Analyze Logs Created by the WWW Service or the FTP Service

Use the following procedure to create a report with Report Writer to analyze logs created by the WWW service or the FTP service:

1. Start Report Writer by selecting Start ➤ Programs ➤ Windows NT 4.0 Option Pack ➤ Site Server 2.0 Express ➤ Report Writer.

2. Accept the From the Report Writer Catalog and click OK.

3. Expand the Detail Reports item.

4. Select Hit detail report and click Next.

5. Accept the Every request you've imported option and click Next.

6. Click Finish.

7. From the Database menu select the Change option.

8. Select the `msusage.mdb` file and click the Open button.

9. Select File ➤ Create Report Document.

10. Enter **defaultweb** in the File Name field and click OK.

11. Click OK.

Exam Essentials

Know how to enable logging for the various services. Enable logging by right-clicking the various services or Web sites in the MMC scope pane, selecting Properties, clicking the Web, FTP, SMTP, or NNTP Site tab, checking Enable Logging, and selecting the log file format.

Key Terms and Concepts

Report Writer: A utility of Site Server Express that summarizes the information contained in IIS logs in a concise human-readable form.

Usage Import: A utility of Site Server Express that translates the log files into a database format understood by Report Writer and retrieves additional information, such as domain name from the IP address.

Sample Questions

1. You want to optimize the content of your Web server, but you don't have a lot of time to spend on the problem. How can you determine which pages deserve the most attention?

   A. Use the Performance Monitor to determine which directories are hit most often.

   B. Use Report Writer to find the 10 most accessed Web pages. Optimize these pages first.

   C. Use Report Writer to identify the most frequent users. Send them e-mail asking which portions of the site deserve the most attention.

   D. Use the Performance Monitor to analyze network performance. When network throughput peaks, use the Server Manager to determine which files are open.

   Answer: B. Report Writer is the fastest way to get summary information.

2. You want to see when during the week your site is most often accessed. Which tool should you use?

   A. Report Writer

   B. Index Server

   C. Content Analyzer

   D. Performance Monitor

   Answer: A. Report Writer will graph how your site has been accessed over a period of time.

Monitor performance of various functions by using Performance Monitor. Functions include HTTP and FTP sessions.

Performance tuning is finding the resource that slows your network the most, speeding it up until something else has the most impact on speed, and then starting over by finding the new slowest resource. This cycle of finding the speed-limiting factor, eliminating it, and starting over allows you to reach the natural performance limit of your network in a simple, methodical way.

Critical Information

Factors that limit performance in a computer are called bottlenecks. For instance, slow memory limits the speed at which a processor can manipulate data, thus limiting the computer's processing performance to the speed that the processor can access memory. If the memory can respond faster than the processor, the processor is the bottleneck. *The* bottleneck in a system is the slowest component, or the component that is causing the other components to wait (even if it is a fast component). Remove that bottleneck (such as by upgrading it) and the next slowest, or heavily loaded, component becomes *the* bottleneck.

System performance is always affected by a bottleneck. You may not notice it because your computer may run faster than the work you perform requires. If you use your computer only for Web service attached to the Internet via a T1 line, the speed of your machine has probably never limited how fast you can work. On the other hand, if you use your computer as an SQL server for a large organization, chances are you've spent a lot of time waiting for the server to catch up to you.

Your connection to the Internet should be your bottleneck in an Internet server. If your server can keep all its connections to the

Internet fully loaded, you're getting all the performance you possibly can out of your Internet server.

Performance tuning Internet servers is the systematic process of finding the resource experiencing the most load and then relieving that load. You can almost always optimize a server to make it more responsive. Understanding how Internet Information Server performs and how you can increase its performance is important. Even if you don't need to make your servers any faster, understanding performance tuning can help you diagnose problems when they arise.

If it's not broken, don't fix it. Windows NT, IIS, and Index Server are highly tuned and factory-optimized to work well in most situations. You should perform rigorous performance monitoring only when a problem that is obviously load-related occurs on your server. You should be especially careful not to cause more harm than good with your performance tuning. Avoid changing any settings or options that you don't fully understand.

Performance tuning is a very complex topic and requires a solid knowledge of the NT operating system, since IIS relies so heavily on it. Ferreting out serious performance problems with the Performance Monitor is beyond the scope of this book.

SEE ALSO   If you need additional information about performance monitoring beyond its use with IIS, check out these books from Sybex: *MCSE: NT Server 4 Study Guide* by Matthew Strebe, Charles Perkins, and James Chellis; *MCSE: NT Workstation 4 Study Guide*, by Charles Perkins, Matthew Strebe, and James Chellis; or *Mastering Windows NT Server 4* by Mark Minasi. Also check out *Optimizing Windows NT,* published by Microsoft Press and included as part of the Windows NT Resource Kit.

The Performance Monitor is the tool built into Windows NT that monitors all facets of its performance. IIS extends the Windows NT Performance Monitor to include unique specialized performance counters for each of the Internet services and for IIS as a whole. This extension of the

Performance Monitor's functionality makes it easy to compare IIS performance counters with Windows NT system counters to find coincidental performance characteristics. Figure 6.3 shows the Performance Monitor running.

F I G U R E 6.3: The Performance Monitor

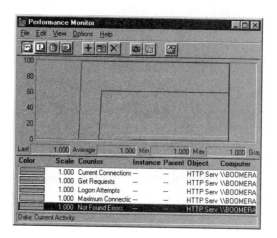

NOTE IIS Services such as the HTTP and FTP services will appear in the Performance Monitor only when the services are running. If you don't see the counter object for the service in the Object pick box, close the Performance Monitor, start the service, and restart the Performance Monitor.

In the following set of counters, each counter counts from the time the service was started, unless otherwise noted by some sort of rate indicator like per second (/sec), current, or percentage (%).

Per second counters measure the number of counts that occur in one second and provide a good indicator of load relative to earlier loads on the same counter. These counters are good for determining the thresholds at which bottlenecks occur and how often those thresholds happen. These can be considered time period counters because they cover a one-second period of time.

Current counters tell you how many instances of a certain load factor are currently occurring—these counters are especially useful for comparing against processor, disk, and memory counters to identify processes that cause bottlenecks to occur. Try putting them on the same charts as processor, disk, and memory counters to find obvious similarities. Using the Performance Monitor this way will help you determine how and when to upgrade your server. These can be considered instantaneous counters because they cover a moment in time.

Counters that don't have a current or per second indicator simply rate the number of times the measured event has occurred since the service was started. Because there's no indication of how long the service has been running, these counters don't mean much in terms of performance monitoring or optimization—but they are a good source for marketing and usage statistics, or as a metric upon which to base fees for services rendered. These are considered time-independent counters because they cover the entire period of time that the service has been running.

TIP You don't have to know about any specific performance counters for the MCSE Exam. However, you should browse through the list of available counters in the Performance Monitor and click the explanation button to see what those counters are for.

Necessary Procedures

Use the following procedure to monitor the performance of the Web service:

1. Select Start ➤ Programs ➤ Administrative Tools ➤ Performance Monitor.

2. Select Edit ➤ Add to Chart or click the large + button on the toolbar.

3. Select Web Service in the Object pick box.

4. Select Current Connections in the Counter list box.

5. Click Add. Note that a colored line has begun moving from right to left in the Performance Monitor main window.

6. Select Web Service in the Object pick box.

7. Select Bytes Total/sec in the Counter list box.

8. Click Add.

9. Click Done. You are now monitoring the number of current connections and the total throughput to the IIS Web service using the Performance Monitor.

Exam Essentials

Understand the purpose of performance monitoring.   Performance monitoring measures performance in order to identify bottlenecks so that appropriate measures can be taken to improve the performance of the machine.

Key Terms and Concepts

Bottleneck: The single most limiting performance factor in a machine.

Counter: A discrete measure of some activity in a computer. Simple counters indicate how many times an event has occurred since the service started. Per second counters indicate how many times per second an event occurs. Current counters indicate the current amount of events that are occurring.

Sample Questions

1. You want to measure how much bandwidth your Web service consumes. Which counter should you monitor?

   A. Memory: Page Output/Sec

   B. IIS Global: Measured Async Bandwidth Usage

   C. Web Service: Bytes Total/Sec

   D. Active Server Pages: Transactions/Sec

   Answer: C. Web Service: Bytes Total/Sec. Other answers are not specific to the Web service.

Analyze performance. Performance issues include:

- Identifying bottlenecks
- Identifying network-related performance issues
- Identifying disk-related performance issues
- Identifying CPU-related performance issues

Critical Information

Now that the Performance Monitor has armed you with knowledge of the internal workings of the IIS services, it's time to actually compare them with other performance counters to determine the impact of the services on the operation of the server. This comparison is the process of performance analysis.

Since IIS isn't the only software running on your computer, many other factors will affect the computer's performance. However, if your server is primarily an Internet or intranet server, most of the performance-affecting software will be engaged in activities directly related to Internet service. If IIS is merely an add-on to a general purpose server that performs everything from file and print service to light SQL duties, you'll have trouble determining which services impact speed the most. If this is the case, perform your testing at night or when the server is mostly idle.

Generate synthetic (meaning made-up or unreal) loads to put the server under a specific sort of strain. For instance, if you want to measure the impact of HTTP service on a general purpose server, isolate the server from other sources of load and then connect a Web browser to a complex Web page twenty or thirty times. This test will put the server under a known load, and you'll be able to filter out how much that specific factor impacts server performance.

Synthetic loads show you how much a specific service loads your system, but they won't ferret out all your performance problems by themselves. Many performance problems don't show up unless the server is under a full load. For instance, let's say you are running an Internet database that has both an Active Server Pages IIS component and an SQL Server component running on the same machine.

Once the server load reaches a certain point, connections start timing out. But which service is causing the problem? A synthetic load won't tell you unless it's designed to exercise both components the same way a real connection would. Even then, you need to determine whether the bottleneck is caused by network I/O, disk, processor, or memory constraints by using performance counters appropriate to those subsystems. You may not be able to overcome a disk bottleneck if both services compete for time on the same disk array—but moving the SQL Server to another machine attached via a fast network fixes the problem completely.

To analyze performance quickly, select the counters that are most relevant to the aspect of performance that you wish to measure (i.e., Memory Allocated if you suspect you are low on memory, Communication Failed and Session Timed Out if you are diagnosing bad connections, or Requests/Second, Requests Current, and Total Queue Length if your server is heavily loaded) and add to the same graph counters for %Processor Time, %Disk time, and Page faults/sec. Now when you put the server under a synthetic Internet service load, you'll see spikes in these counters that correspond directly to the service counters you added. This measurement gives you a good indication of the relative load IIS is causing on your machine for a specific level of concurrent use.

Many serious performance problems are sporadic. You may have to use the Alerting or Logging features of IIS to track down strange or infrequent problems, or problems that tend to occur when you aren't around. These features are beyond the scope of this book, but you should be able to figure out how to use them with the help file built into the Performance Monitor.

Necessary Procedures

To generate a small synthetic load:

1. Double-click the Internet Explorer icon on your desktop.

2. Arrange the positions of Internet Explorer and the Performance Monitor on your desktop so you can see the content windows of both of them at the same time. You may need to make Internet Explorer very small.

3. Type //*computername*/default.htm in the Address input line, replacing *computername* with the name of your Internet server.

4. Notice the slight load this action creates on your server. Also notice that the load drops back down after the initial connection once the page is loaded. This example shows the "bursty" nature of HTTP transmissions.

Exam Essentials

Understand the methodology for identifying and resolving bottlenecks. You identify bottlenecks by comparing counters either to establish baseline normal values or by monitoring the effect of counters that indicate failures. When counters indicate a bottleneck other than the network connection, software should be made more efficient or hardware should be upgraded.

Key Terms and Concepts

Synthetic load: Activity of a fixed and known amount engaged in specifically for the purpose of measuring a computer's ability to respond to it.

Sample Questions

1. Users are complaining that Web pages are taking a lot longer to load than they used to. Using the Performance Monitor, you determine that your intranet server is bandwidth-limited because it is attached to your network via a single Ethernet network adapter. Which repairs are appropriate? (Choose all that apply.)

   A. Use throttling to restrict bandwidth to the amount supported by the network link.

   B. Upgrade the link technology to fast Ethernet.

   C. Implement disk striping to speed access to the Web pages.

   D. Upgrade to the latest version of IIS, which is faster than previous versions.

   E. Optimize the content on your site by making images smaller, eliminating graphical content when possible, and providing text-only pages for people who don't care to see images.

   Answer: B, E. If you are bandwidth-limited, you can either speed up the connection or transmit less information.

Optimize performance of IIS.

O ptimizing the performance of IIS is the most important step to optimizing your Internet server, because IIS generates the majority of traffic (and therefore performance-related problems) on your server.

Critical Information

There are numerous ways to optimize the performance of IIS. Chief among them are:

- limiting user connections
- enabling HTTP Keep-Alives
- bandwidth throttling

Limiting user connections is a simple optimization—by reducing the number of users who can connect to your site, you improve performance for those who are connected because they don't have to compete for bandwidth with as many users. Network traffic to a single server is a "divide by N" problem because the available bandwidth is divided by the number of users connected. If you have a 1500Kbps connection with 100 users attached, you have 1500Kbps/100 (1500Kbps) available for each user. If you limit connections to only 10 users, each user will have 1500Kbps/10 available (150Kbps)—a ten times increase in performance.

Why would you want to limit the number of users to your site? Because with too many users, your server will become so slow that it's worthless to everyone. It's better to be able to fill the needs of some users at least.

HTTP Keep-Alives improve performance by maintaining the connection to the Web browser so IIS can more quickly respond to multiple HTTP requests to the same browser. HTTP Keep-Alives do, however, require more resources when enabled, so there's a performance trade-off. If your computer is resource-limited (for example, if it has only 32 megabytes of RAM), you might want to disable HTTP Keep-Alives. Each open connection takes up some memory, so disabling the Keep-Alives frees up server resources—but also causes subsequent HTTP requests from Web browsers to take longer (a new connection must be negotiated for each request).

Bandwidth throttling lets you determine how much of your network resources you want consumed by each specific Web site. Throttling bandwidth to a Web or FTP site does not make that site perform better. In fact, metering bandwidth impedes performance by restricting load times to a certain level. It can, however, improve the performance of other Web or FTP sites on your server if that site is "hogging" all of the available network bandwidth. Also, if you are using IIS on a server that does double duty as a file server and the IIS traffic is simply not as important as the regular network traffic, you may have to use bandwidth metering to prevent Internet traffic from stealing time away from more important uses of your machine.

Your pipe to the Internet is an automatic bandwidth meter. If you have a 56K leased line, your Internet traffic will never account for more than 56K of network I/O. You don't have to set anything for inherent bottlenecks like this to limit the flow of information to and from your server.

You can also throttle bandwidth globally by enabling bandwidth throttling on the IIS Master Properties page. This will limit the traffic consumed by all IIS services rather than by Web site.

Necessary Procedures

Use the following procedure to limit the number of users who can connect to a Web site:

1. Start the Internet Service Manager.

2. Right-click the site you want to limit and select Properties.

3. Select the Web Site tab.

4. Select Limit To and enter **100** in the Connections input box.

5. Click OK.

Use the following procedure to enable HTTP Keep-Alives:

1. Start the Internet Service Manager.

2. Right-click the site you want to modify and select Properties.

3. Select the Performance tab.

4. Check the HTTP Keep-Alives Enabled option.

5. Click OK.

Use the following procedure to meter bandwidth for a specific Web site:

1. Start the Internet Service Manager.

2. Right-click the site you want to limit and select Properties.

3. Select the Performance tab.

4. Check the Enable Bandwidth Throttling option.

5. Enter the amount of Kbps you want that site to be limited to.

6. Click Apply.

7. Click OK.

Exam Essentials

Understand how limiting connections improves performance.
Limiting connections improves performance by ensuring that a server cannot become so bogged down by connections that it cannot effectively respond to clients. This is analogous to limiting the number of cars on the freeway to prevent traffic jams.

Understand how HTTP Keep-Alives affects performance. HTTP Keep-Alives hold the TCP connection open between page requests, thus obviating the time and compute resources necessary to re-establish the connection for each successive access to the same server. However, since there's no clear indication of when a browser will no longer request pages, the connection will always be kept alive longer than necessary, which could use up valuable memory resources on memory-limited machines.

Understand how bandwidth throttling optimizes performance.
Bandwidth throttling optimizes server performance by ensuring that heavily trafficked Web sites can't swamp the resources of a machine. Bandwidth can be allocated on a per–Web site basis, and can also be limited for all IIS services combined to prevent Internet services from swamping a machine that has other duties.

Key Terms and Concepts

Bandwidth throttling: The apportioning of bandwidth among the various Web sites or services on an Internet server.

HTTP Keep-Alives: An optimization that holds open TCP/IP connections when they would normally be closed to obviate the overhead of reestablishing the connection.

Sample Questions

1. With Report Writer you determine that one Web site (containing free downloads) is using 10 times the bandwidth that your commercial (subscription) site is using. Subscription customers are complaining. What can you do to ensure that the commercial site gets preference?

   A. Limit the number of simultaneous connections accepted by the download site.

   B. Limit the number of simultaneous connections accepted by the commercial site.

   C. Limit the bandwidth of the download site.

   D. Limit the bandwidth of the commercial site.

   Answer: C. Limiting the bandwidth of the download site gives preference to the commercial users.

2. You want to monitor the number of connections made to your IIS computer in real time. Which tool would you use?

   A. Report Writer

   B. Index Server

   C. Content Analyzer

   D. Performance Monitor

   Answer: D. Performance Monitor will graph the number of connections for you in real time and compare them to other operating system values.

Optimize performance of Index Server.

Index Server is highly optimized and tuned for near-maximum performance upon installation. However, there are a few things you can do to improve the performance of Index Server in your specific environment.

Critical Information

The Index Server search engine is designed for speed efficiency. When indexed documents change on a server, they are added to a change queue. The change queue is processed in first-in, first-out order very shortly after the documents are stored.

When documents are first indexed, the resulting index of words is stored in RAM in a buffer called a word list. Word lists are not compressed, and they are stored only in RAM, so they can be stored very quickly. When the size of a word list reaches a certain point, it is compressed and stored into a shadow index on the disk. Shadow indexes serve as disk buffers for word lists that have not yet been added to the monolithic master index. Shadow indexes are easy to create but do cause a small amount of disk and processor load. A shadow merge combines all the shadow indexes and word lists into a single shadow index whenever the number of word lists or shadow indexes passes a certain threshold. Shadow merges are generally very fast because the indexes are small.

The master index is the main index for all the documents indexed by the search engine. Every night at midnight (by default) a shadow merge occurs to combine all the word lists and indexes into a single shadow index. Then a master merge occurs to add the shadow index changes to the master index.

All this effort with word lists, shadow indexes, and merges is an important optimization because adding words to the master index is very time-consuming. If every document index were master-merged after each indexing during the day, the load on your server would be tremendous. Word lists and shadow indexes serve as caches for the master merge so that the load-intensive master merge can be delayed until the server is under a light load.

The trade-off for this load optimization is query speed. Every query has to first search all existing word lists, then all shadow indexes, and then the master index each time it is performed. Searching only the master index is much faster, so queries are quicker after a master merge.

TIP Be sure you understand the performance improvement master merges will give your query speed.

The NT Server Performance Monitor utility can be used to determine how your Index Server is loaded using the following objects:

- Content Index
- Content Index Filter
- HTTP Content Index

These objects show you the current state of merges, the number of persistent indexes in your system, and the number and size of word lists. By relating these values to the disk, memory, and processor loads in your system, you can determine how much load Index Server puts on your system. Try staying up one night and monitoring your server's performance during a master merge. You will learn a lot about the indexing load your server is subject to, which will help you make determinations about how to optimize index speed.

If your server spends more time on queries than on merges, you should tighten up the registry values to force merges more often. On the other hand, if your server is spending too much time on merges, you should loosen up the intervals between master merges. Examine the Registry Settings page in the Index Server online documentation very carefully for a complete list of registry keys that can be modified to tune the performance of Index Server.

The following Index Server optimizations are especially effective. You should check out the Index Server online documentation for specific information on how to perform some of these optimizations:

- Move a catalog to a different hard disk than the corpus. (The corpus is all the files that are indexed in a catalog.) This optimization splits the I/O traffic during the master merge among two disks and eliminates the need to seek the disk head between the areas containing the corpus and the areas containing the index.

- Use the standard Windows NT speed optimizations like striped hard disks or hardware RAID arrays to improve disk I/O speed on servers that hold the corpus.

- Increase the amount of RAM in your computer. You can edit registry settings to allow larger word lists in RAM, thus lengthening the time to the next shadow merge.

- Create multiple catalogs if you don't need the ability to query everything at once. For instance, you may want to create separate catalogs for office documents and for HTML files, because users will generally know what type of document they are searching for. Smaller indexes mean faster searches.

- Narrow the scope of your queries by eliminating virtual directories that don't contain useful query information, such as scripts directories and directories that contain ISAPI applications or Java code.

- Change the time that the daily master merge takes place to coincide with the time of day when your server is under the least load. If you are running a public Internet server, this time is most likely in the early morning between 4 A.M. and 9 A.M.; however, if you get browsers from all over the world, there may be no ideal time for this procedure.

- Set Index Server to filter only files with known file types. This setting keeps a lot of garbage files out of your query indexes and makes everything run quite a bit faster.

Check out the registry Settings page in the Index Server online documentation for a complete list of the registry settings that you can modify to optimize Index Server.

SEE ALSO Check out *MCSE: Internet Information Server 4 Study Guide* by Matthew Strebe and Charles Perkins (Sybex, 1998) for more information on Index Server.

Index Server installs a number of performance counters that can be viewed using either the NT Server Performance Monitor or a Web browser. The HTML Index Server Manager automatically shows relevant statistics on the main page when you open it (see Figure 6.4).

F I G U R E 6.4: The HTML Index Server Manager

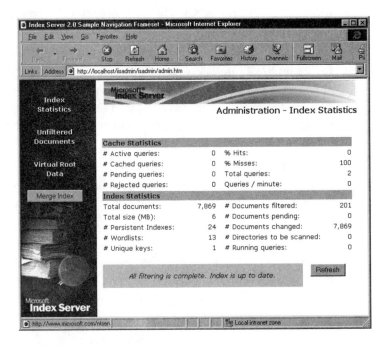

Necessary Procedures

Use the following procedure to add Index Server counters to the Performance Monitor:

1. Select Start ➤ Programs ➤ Administrative Tools ➤ Performance Monitor.

2. Click the + button to add a counter to the Performance Monitor display.

3. Select **Content Index** in the Object pick list.

4. Select **#documents filtered** in the Counter pick list.

5. Click Add.

6. Select Start ➤ Settings ➤ Control Panel.

7. Double-click the Services control panel.

8. Select the Content Index service.

9. Click the Stop button. Wait for the service to stop.

10. Click the Start button.

11. Click the Performance Monitor button in the task bar.

12. Notice the indexed documents counter climb. Listen for disk activity on your server.

13. Close the Performance Monitor, the Services control panel, and the Control Panel windows.

Exam Essentials

Understand the concept of merges.   Merging is the process of moving indexed words successively from the RAM-based word list to the shadow indexes, merging them into a monolithic shadow index, and then moving them into the master index. These levels of caching improve the performance of Index Server by staving off the time-consuming process of adding words to the master index until a more convenient time when the server is under lighter load.

Key Terms and Concepts

Corpus: The body of files that are indexed in a catalog.

Master index: The main index for all the documents indexed by the search engine.

Master merge: An operation that merges the shadow index into the master index.

Shadow indexes: Disk buffers for word lists that have not yet been added to the monolithic master index.

Shadow merge: An operation that combines all the shadow indexes and word lists into a single shadow index whenever the number of word lists or shadow indexes passes a certain threshold.

Word List: A RAM buffer used to store indexed words until they are merged into the catalog.

Sample Questions

1. Index Server queries are taking too long. You've already restricted queries to the file types you actually want queried, but because of heavy usage, the Index Server is still not able to keep up. Using the Performance Monitor, you determine that shadow merges and master merges are happening far too often because new documents are being updated frequently. Which optimizations will help? (Choose all that apply.)

   A. Increase the amount of disk space allocated for shadow merges.

   B. Change the default master merge time to occur at 4:00 A.M. when the network is less loaded.

   C. Increase the amount of disk space allocated to catalogs.

D. Implement bandwidth throttling to limit the number of simultaneous queries.

E. Install more RAM and increase the amount of memory reserved for word lists to decrease frequency of shadow merges and master merges.

F. Move the catalog to a disk different than the corpus to reduce the time that merges take to execute.

Answer: B, E, and F. Increasing the amount of RAM allocated to word lists will increase time between merges, and moving the catalog will reduce the time that merges take to execute. Scheduling the master merge to occur in off hours also improves performance.

Optimize performance of Microsoft SMTP Service.

The steps you take to optimize IIS and the Web service will help you to optimize the other Internet services as well. Metering the bandwidth to greedy Web sites can give your SMTP site room to breathe.

Critical Information

The Mail service, like the Web service, logs access. You configure the log files in the same way you configure the Web service log files, and you can import those log files into a spreadsheet or database tool to analyze them for trends in how your Internet site is being used.

Logging in the Mail service gives you the same four format options as the Web service—Microsoft IIS Log File Format, NCSA Common Log File Format, ODBC Logging, and the W3C Extended Log File Format. As with the Web service, the W3C format allows you to select the data that will be included in the log file.

In addition to log data, the Mail service has counters that you can view in the Performance Monitor. You can use these counters to monitor trends in the behavior of these services and to solve performance problems.

A few things you can do to improve Mail performance include:

- Limit the number of simultaneous connections to the Mail service. This gives connected users more bandwidth and processor capacity at the expense of denying connections to other users, making them wait until the site is less busy.

- Decrease the connection timeout for the Mail services so that other users can connect and use the (insignificant) bandwidth and (significant) memory taken by idle connections.

- Disable logging (only do this if you need every last bit of performance).

- Decrease the maximum number of messages per connection in the SMTP service, which will cause it to open more connections and deliver mail faster. You can also decrease the retry interval for local and remote mail delivery—this instructs the SMTP service to try again sooner. Increasing the retry interval has a negative effect on the bandwidth available, though, so don't do it if you are bandwidth-limited. Turn off reverse DNS lookup for incoming messages.

By now, you should have a pretty good feel for the various performance-related features of the various IIS services including SMTP.

Necessary Procedures

Use the following procedure to decrease the maximum number of messages per SMTP connection, thereby forcing SMTP to open more connections:

1. Launch the MMC.

2. Right-click on the SMTP service and select Properties.

3. Select the Messages tab.

4. Select Maximum number of outbound message per connection.

5. Enter a low value (such as **10**) in the box.

6. Click OK.

Exam Essentials

Know how to improve the performance of SMTP. Decreasing the number of messages per connection will improve SMTP performance by causing it to open multiple simultaneous TPC/IP connections to the receiving host.

Key Terms and Concepts

Message: An addressed text message that is transmitted electronically from one server to another. E-mail.

Sample Questions

1. Choose the sequence that enables SMTP service transaction logs to create a new log every month using the Microsoft IIS log file format:

   A. Select the Default SMTP Site, select Action ➤ Properties, check Enable Logging, click OK.

   B. Select the local host, select Action ➤ Properties, select SMTP Service in the Master Properties pick box, check Enable Logging, select Microsoft IIS Log File Format, click OK.

   C. Select the default SMTP Site, select Action ➤ Properties, select SMTP Service in the Master Properties pick box, check Enable Logging, select Microsoft IIS Log File Format, click Properties, select Monthly, click OK, click OK.

D. Select the local host, select Action ➤ Properties, select SMTP Service in the Master Properties pick box, check Enable Logging, select Microsoft IIS Log File Format, click OK.

Answer: C. Other options either don't work or do not complete the requirement.

Optimize performance of Microsoft NNTP Service.

Critical Information

The performance optimization features discussed for the other services also apply to NNTP. In addition to those methods, you can use the following optimizations that are somewhat specific to NNTP.

Limit the post size to prevent users from hogging space and bandwidth. Large posts take a long time to transmit and take a lot of space on your NNTP server. For most NNTP servers, there's no valid reason why large posts should be accepted.

Limit connection size to prevent NNTP from hogging bandwidth. NNTP allows you to limit the amount of bandwidth a single NNTP connection will be allowed to use. You can do this to prevent NNTP from consuming too much bandwidth at any one time.

Use virtual directories to store newsgroups on different hard disks. Virtual directories allow you to put newsgroups on other volumes and on other servers. If you have the rare occasion to run a disk-limited NNTP server, spread newsgroups onto other disks to improve performance.

Necessary Procedures

Use the following procedure to create an NNTP virtual directory on another volume. This exercise only works if you have an additional writable storage device mounted as drive D:

1. Launch the MMC.

2. Right-click the default NNTP Site and click New ➤ Virtual Directory.

3. Enter a newsgroup to store in the virtual directory (for example, **hr.policies**) and press Enter.

4. Enter a path located on another physical disk, such as **d:\hr**, and press Enter.

5. Click Yes to create the new directory.

Exam Essentials

Understand the NNTP specific performance optimizations. You can use the virtual directories feature to balance your news load among several drives or even among several servers if necessary.

Key Terms and Concepts

Virtual directory: A method to link outside directories into the served directory hierarchy of an IIS service, thus allowing Web sites, NNTP sites, and FTP sites to be spread across multiple disks or servers.

Sample Questions

1. Create a virtual directory for the NNTP service to store trouble-shooting tips in the g:\tips directory. Choose the correct sequence:

   A. Right-click the NNTP site, select New ➤ Virtual Directory, enter **Troubleshooting Tips** in the Newsgroup Name, click Next, enter **g:\tips**, click Finish.

   B. Right-click the NNTP site, select Properties, select the Directories tab, click New, enter **Troubleshooting Tips** as the newsgroup name, click Next, enter **g:\tips**, click Finish.

   C. Right-click the NNTP site, select Properties, select Groups, click Create New Newsgroup, enter **Troubleshooting Tips** as the newsgroup name, click OK.

   D. Right-click the NNTP site, select Properties, select Groups, click Create New Newsgroup, enter **Troubleshooting Tips** as the newsgroup name, enter **g:\tips** in the path input box, click OK.

   Answer: A. C creates a newsgroup in the root directory, and the other options won't work.

Interpret performance data.

Information for this objective is contained under the Analyze performance objective.

Critical Information

There is no critical information for this objective.

Necessary Procedures

There are no necessary procedures for this objective.

Exam Essentials

There are no exam essentials for this objective.

Key Terms and Concepts

There are no key terms or concepts for this objective.

Sample Questions

There are no sample questions for this objective.

Optimize a Web site by using Content Analyzer.

The Content Analyzer is the tool you use to manage what is stored in the directories of your Web site (unlike the Microsoft Management Console, which concerns itself primarily with the directories themselves and how the browser connects to them). Content Analyzer allows you to easily optimize the content of your Web site rather than the Web server service.

SEE ALSO There is additional information relevant to this objective in Chapter 3 under "Manage a Web site by using Content Analyzer."

Critical Information

A Web map is a graphical view of the resources in a Web site. When you create a Web map, Site Server Express traverses all of the HTML pages it can find in the Web site and records those pages as well as all of the objects (graphics, sounds, external pages, etc.) that those pages reference. The information about the Web site is stored in a .wmp file so that the Web site needn't be traversed every time you want to use Site Server Express.

Site Server Express can traverse a Web site in two ways:

- WebMaps from URLs
- WebMaps from files

If Site Server Express is running on a different computer than IIS4, you will probably connect to the Web site using the Web site's URL. Site Server Express will use the HTTP protocol to connect to the site and gather its information.

When you create a WebMap, you can set constraints and options to limit how extensive your WebMap will be and hence how much space it will take up and how much of a load it will place on a remote (URL-accessed) Web site. In addition, you can instruct Site Server Express to make a local copy of the Web site.

In order to create a WebMap from a URL, you simply provide the URL path to the home page of the Web site (see Figure 6.5). You can instruct Site Server to explore the entire site, to organize the WebMap by directory hierarchy rather than the order in which links are found, and to generate a site report automatically as it creates the WebMap. If you do not want Site Server Express to explore the entire site, you will be able to choose how many pages will be explored. When Site Server Express is done exploring the site, it will ask you for a name prefix for the summary report and (if you instructed it to generate a report) show you summary statistics for the Web site.

FIGURE 6.5: You can map a site over the Internet by providing a URL

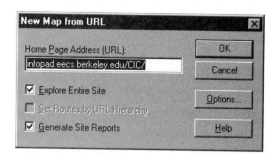

If the Web site is stored locally (either on the same computer as Site Server Express or on another computer in your LAN), you can point Site Server Express to the directory path or UNC path to the Web (see Figure 6.6).

FIGURE 6.6: If the Web site resides on your hard drive you can create the Web map by specifying directory locations

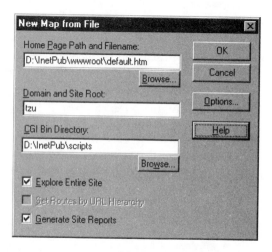

As with creating a URL-sourced WebMap, with a directly accessed Web site you can set constraints and options to limit how extensive your WebMap will be, including whether it will access off-site links and which URLs it will not explore. In addition, you can instruct Site Server Express to explore all of the content of the Web site directories, rather than just the content referenced by hyperlinks. This is an excellent way to find orphaned Web pages.

In order to create a WebMap from files, you must provide the following:

- a home page path and filename (this may be a UNC path or a standard pathname starting with a drive letter)

- a domain and site root (this may be the Internet name of the Web site)

- the location of the CGI Bin directory used by the Web site (specified the same way you specified the home page path and filename)

You can instruct Site Server to explore the entire site, to organize the WebMap by directory hierarchy (rather than the order in which links are found), and to generate a site report automatically as it creates the WebMap. If you do not want Site Server Express to explore the entire site, you will be able to choose how many pages will be explored. When Site Server Express is done exploring the site, it will ask you for a name prefix for the summary report and (if you instructed it to generate a report) show you summary statistics for the Web site.

Site Server Express creates a summary report by default (unless you uncheck the Summary Report checkbox) and displays it in your Web browser when you create an initial WebMap. Microsoft Site Server (the commercial version, which is not included with Internet Information Server 4) has additional reports that can tell you more about your Web site. The summary report is divided into three parts:

- **Object Statistics**   This part lists the number and size of the objects stored in your Web site, broken down by their type (such as HTML pages, Java classes, image files, and so on).

- **Status Summary**   This part describes the links in your Web site, separated into on-site and off-site links, and shows the number of good links, bad links, missing links, and unverified links.

- **Map Statistics**   This part gives you such information as when the map was made, how "deep" it got, and the average number of links on a page in the Web site.

A graphic view of your links is a neat tool, but the real benefit of Site Server Express is its ability to search your Web map for problems such as broken links, "not found" objects, images without ALT tags, and large objects (which can cause a page to take a very long time to download). The Tools menu gives you the option to do a quick search on the following objects:

- Broken Links

- Home Site Objects

- Images Without ALT

- Load Size over 32K

- Non-Home Site Objects

- Not Found Objects (404)

- Unavailable Objects

- Unverified Objects

When you search on any one of these objects, Site Server Express creates a search results window and lists those objects in it. When you click on the object in the search results window, the tree view and cyberbolic view automatically go to that object. You can then double-click on the object (or its parent if it is a broken link or a not-found object) to view the problem object or HTML page.

Site Server Express makes finding broken links easy. Then it is just a matter of fixing that link with the software you used to create the page, or perhaps just editing the file with a text editor so that the link points to the correct location. You need to set Verify offsite links if you want Site Server Express to make sure links outside your site are valid, because it does not verify them by default.

NOTE Site Server Express, unfortunately, does not give you the capability to search for user-defined text, including searching for the content of hypertext links, headings, or titles. If you want to search for these items you must purchase Site Analyst. Site Analyst is a feature of Microsoft Site Server 2 and Microsoft Site Server, Enterprise Edition 2.

Necessary Procedures

To create a WebMab from a file and configure Content Analyzer:

1. Select Start ➤ Programs ➤ Administrative Tools ➤ Windows NT 4 Option Pack ➤ Site Server Express 2.0 ➤ Content Analyzer to start the Content Analyzer.

2. Click the New WebMap button.

3. Select File and click OK.

4. Enter the home page path and filename of the default Web site home page (`c:\inetpub\wwwroot\index.htm` for most installations).

5. Enter the domain site and root (the name of your server).

6. Enter the location of the Scripts directory for the location of the CGI Bin directory (`c:\inetpub\scripts` for most installations).

7. Click OK.

8. Click OK in the Generate Site Reports window.

9. Observe the Server Summary report and then close the report (browser) window.

10. Select View ➤ Program Options.

11. Click the Cyberbolic tab.

12. Check the Enable Snap Mode option.

13. Uncheck the Show Common Ancestor When Selecting In Tree View option.

14. Click Apply.

15. Click OK.

Exam Essentials

Understand the sort of information Content Analyzer can provide to help optimize your Web sites.   Content Analyzer helps you ferret out problem Web content like large files, links that point to nonexistent files, and orphaned files that take up space but are not referenced in your site.

Key Terms and Concepts

Summary Report: An HTML page generated by Content Analyzer containing the details you need to optimize your Web site contents.

Web map: A graphical view of the relationships between HTML pages in a Web site.

Sample Questions

1. Which tool will most quickly help you find all the broken links in your Web site?

  A. Report Writer

  B. Index Server

  C. Content Analyzer

  D. Performance Monitor

  Answer: C. Content Analyzer can search a Web map to find all the broken links in your site.

CHAPTER

7

Troubleshooting

Microsoft Exam Objectives Covered in This Chapter:

▶ **Resolve IIS configuration problems.** *(pages 252 – 254)*

▶ **Resolve security problems.** *(pages 254 – 258)*

▶ **Resolve resource access problems.** *(pages 259 – 262)*

▶ **Resolve Index Server query problems.** *(pages 262 – 266)*

▶ **Resolve setup issues when installing IIS on a Windows NT Server 4.0 computer.** *(pages 266 – 270)*

▶ **Use a WebMap to find and repair broken links.** *(pages 270 – 274)*

▶ **Resolve WWW service problems.** *(pages 274 – 279)*

▶ **Resolve FTP service problems.** *(pages 280 – 284)*

Resolve IIS configuration problems.

Very few errors apply just to the configuration of IIS itself—IIS installs automatically and very cleanly, so there's very little that can actually go wrong under normal circumstances.

Critical Information

If, however, your IIS installation becomes corrupted, the following troubleshooting steps should be used in the order shown:

1. Delete and re-create problem Web sites. If the problem you're experiencing occurs only for a single Web site, and you've exhausted other troubleshooting measures, try deleting the site in the MMC and re-creating it. This often repairs metabase or registry corruption.

2. Reapply the latest service pack. Some software automatically installs older versions of system DLLs which can cause compatibility problems with applications like IIS that rely upon the services of the most recent system software. Reapplying the service pack generally resolves these problems.

3. Reinstall IIS4. Reinstalling IIS4 will restore missing files, registry keys, and metabase settings, automatically fixing a number of otherwise perplexing problems.

4. Remove IIS4 completely and reinstall. Sometimes registry or metabase settings become corrupt and the corruption persists through IIS4 installations. In these cases, you may have to completely remove IIS4 before reinstalling it to correct the problem.

See the Critical Information sections of the remaining objectives in this chapter for further information about IIS configuration problems.

Necessary Procedures

See the necessary procedures for other objectives throughout this chapter.

Exam Essentials

There are no exam essentials for this objective.

Key Terms and Concepts

Registry corruption: Any state where conflicting registry information exists or where registry information is missing such that the proper operation of services is not possible. Often, reinstallation of software is required to properly restore registry settings.

Sample Questions

There are no sample questions for this objective.

Resolve security problems.

Web sites and FTP sites are easy to set up using IIS, and both IIS and NTFS security are very effective at protecting your data. You have to be careful when establishing security for your Internet site, however, because you can configure things so securely that even you can't access them.

Critical Information

When setting up security for a site, keep the following in mind:

- Secure posting requires Secure Socket Layer, so you must have SSL configured and working on a Web site before you can use secure posting.

- Permissions for the anonymous user are controlled by adding NTFS permissions for the IUSR_*computername* account or the account specified in the Directory Security Anonymous Security and Authentication Control area of the Web site's properties.

- You can specify the anonymous user for each Web site through the Directory Security Anonymous Security and Authentication button in the Web site's properties.

- You can restrict access to or from a Web site by specific IP addresses or IP networks through the Directory Security IP Address and Domain Name Restrictions area of the Web site's properties.

- Service security restrictions control read access, write access, script execution, and application execution per site irrespective of user identity. When you need to control security for all users of a site, use service-based restrictions. Use NTFS permissions when various users will be allowed different levels of access.

- Restrict write access to Web, FTP, and NNTP sites that do not allow uploading or posting.

Use the following pointers when troubleshooting security problems with an IIS installation:

- **Can't automatically submit a certificate request to Certificate Server.** Certificate Server must be installed and running on your computer (or on another computer in your network).

- **Can't require SSL communications on a Home Directory or Virtual Directory.** You must have a signed certificate installed in order to require Secure Socket Layer communications. You must have Windows NT Challenge/Response enabled to require Secure Socket Layer communications.

- **Can't audit NTFS file and directory activity.** You must have auditing enabled in the User Manager or User Manager for Domains program.

- **IIS will not execute a script or DLL.** Script or Execute permissions must be enabled in a Home Directory or Virtual Directory before IIS will execute the program.

- **Users cannot log on using Basic Authentication but are able to using Windows NT Challenge/Response.** Basic Authentication must be enabled for users to log on using a specific account without using Windows NT Challenge/Response. In a multi-domain network, the default domain configured for Basic Authentication must be the domain from which all Basic users will be authenticated.

- **Users from outside your firewall cannot access Web sites on non-standard port addresses (such as the Administration Web site).** Your firewall must be configured to pass specific non-standard port numbers.

- **Users are confronted with a logon prompt even when they want to log on anonymously.** Logging on without a logon prompt or Windows NT Challenge/Response requires that Anonymous Authentication be enabled. The NTFS permissions for the files accessed must also include the anonymous user account.

- **Users report that they get a logon prompt when they attempt to access the Web site but access is denied after they enter an account name and password.** You must have an account defined for the users if Anonymous Authentication is disabled.

- **You can't log on to the IIS Administrative Web site.** You must have Windows NT Challenge/Response enabled to use the administrative Web pages.

- **The anonymous user cannot access any files.** The anonymous account defined in the Web site Authentication Properties sheet must also exist, have the Log on locally user right, and have the same password as a Windows NT account. Ensure password synchronization is enabled. Anonymous accounts must be set to Password Never Expires.

- **Browsers other than Internet Explorer are unable to be authenticated by your Web site.** Web browsers other than Internet Explorer require Basic Authentication to be authenticated as anything other than an anonymous user.

- **Users can't access Web site data stored on UNC share.** Be sure that share permissions are set correctly, and that an account name and password are established for Web site access to the share.

With the myriad shares, groups, files, and directories that can be created in a network environment, some resource permission conflicts are bound to occur. When a user is a member of many groups, some of those groups may specifically allow access to a resource while other group memberships deny it. Also, cumulative permissions may occur. For example, a user may have Read access to a directory because he's a domain user and also have Full Control because he's a member of the Engineers group. Windows NT determines access privileges in the following manner:

- A specific denial (the No Access permission) always overrides specific access to a resource.

- When resolving conflicts between share permissions and file permissions, Windows NT chooses the most restrictive. For instance, if the share permission allows full control but the file permissions allow read-only, the file is read-only.

- When a user is a member of multiple groups, the user always has the combined permissions of all group memberships and any individual permissions assigned to the User Account.

Necessary Procedures

Use the following procedure to enable password synchronization for a Web site:

1. Right-click the default Web site in the MMC and select Properties.

2. Select the Directory Security tab.

3. Click Edit in the Anonymous Access and Authentication Control area.

4. Check Allow Anonymous Access and click Edit.

5. Click Browse.

6. Select the IUSR_*computername* account for this server, or another account if you want to use a different account for anonymous access.

7. Check Enable Automatic Password Synchronization.

8. Click OK.

9. Click Yes to continue.

10. Click OK.

11. Click OK.

Exam Essentials

Understand the purpose of password synchronization and how to enable it. Password synchronization prevents the anonymous logon failures caused when the anonymous user account's password is changed. Enable this feature through the Directory Security properties of a Web site.

Key Terms and Concepts

Password synchronization: IIS's ability to automatically update the IIS services with the passwords of anonymous user accounts, thus preventing anonymous users from being denied Web pages if the IUSR_*computername* account password is changed.

Sample Questions

1. Anonymous users cannot access your Web site. Which of the following reasons might explain why?

   A. The anonymous account defined in the Web site Authentication Properties sheet does not exist.

   B. The anonymous account defined in the Web site Authentication Properties sheet does not have the Log on locally user right.

   C. The anonymous account defined in the Web site Authentication Properties sheet does not have the same password as the Windows NT account.

   D. The anonymous account defined in the Web site Authentication Properties sheet does not have password synchronization enabled.

   E. The anonymous account defined in the Web site Authentication Properties sheet is not set to Password Never Expires.

   Answer: A, B, C, D, and **E.** Each of these conditions must be corrected to ensure trouble-free anonymous user support.

Resolve resource access problems.

Access problems occur when a server can't be located or when security settings prevent authorized users from gaining access.

Critical Information

Access problems for Web sites fall into the following categories:

- **Connection problems** occur when no physical path to the destination server exists. These problems are quite obvious but beyond the scope of this book and the exam.

SEE ALSO   Refer to *MCSE: Networking Essentials Study Guide* by James Chellis, Charles Perkins, and Matthew Strebe (Sybex, 1998) for information on troubleshooting connection problems.

- **Routing problems** occur when TCP/IP packets cannot flow between the client and the server due to problems with routing tables, which are rare and outside the scope of this book and the exam.

SEE ALSO   Refer to *MCSE: TCP/IP Study Guide* by Todd Lammle, Monica Lammle, and James Chellis (Sybex, 1997) for information on troubleshooting routing problems.

- **Name resolution problems** occur when your browser cannot resolve the name provided in the URL to the IP address of the correct server. To find your Web site, the browser must be running on a computer that knows the IP address of a DNS server that can resolve your domain name, or a WINS server that knows your server's friendly name. To troubleshoot name resolution, make sure the client TCP/IP stack is set correctly to point to a WINS or DNS server, and make sure that the WINS or DNS server is properly providing your server's IP address.

SEE ALSO Name resolution is covered in greater detail in *MCSE: Internet Information Server 4 Study Guide* by Matthew Strebe and Charles Perkins (Sybex, 1998).

- **Security problems** occur when the client cannot provide credentials that satisfy the server. To secure Web access from anonymous Web browsers and force Internet users to log in, remove the IUSR_ *computername* account from the NTFS permissions for the Web site files. Make sure no groups that the IUSR account is a member of are in the permission list (such as EVERYONE). Anonymous users won't be able to log in unless you enter the correct password for the selected account or enable password synchronization in the Directory Security Anonymous Security and Authentication button in the Web site's properties.

SEE ALSO Security for Web sites is covered in greater detail in *MCSE: Internet Information Server 4 Study Guide* and in *NT Network Security* by Matthew Strebe, Charles Perkins, and Michael Moncur (Sybex, 1998).

Necessary Procedures

Use the following permissions to force a user to log on before using the default Web site:

1. Browse to `c:\inetpub\wwwroot` or its equivalent on your machine using the desktop Explorer.

2. Right-click on `default.asp` and select Properties.

3. Select Security.

4. Click Permissions.

5. Select the Everyone/Full Control permission and click Remove.

6. Select the IUSR_*computername* permission and click Remove.

7. Click Add.

8. Select Domain Users and click Add.

9. Select Full Control and click OK.

10. Click OK.

11. Click OK.

Exam Essentials

Know how to force an Internet user to log into your Web site.
Removing the IUSR_*computername* account from the ACL of your Web site files will force the client to log in. Their Web browser will display a dialog requesting a logon name and password. Only Internet Explorer is compatible with Windows NT Challenge/Response authentication; other Web browsers use Basic Authentication.

Know how to allow anonymous users access to your site.   Add the IUSR_*computername* account to the ACL of your Web site files to allow anonymous users and prevent the logon dialog from being displayed on their Web browsers.

Key Terms and Concepts

Name Resolution: The process of resolving the network layer address of a computing device given its name. Domain Name Service looks the name up in a distributed database managed by name servers. NetBIOS-based networking protocols use broadcasts and dynamic discovery to record the names of computers participating in the same broadcast domain.

Sample Questions

1. You've created a Web site where users can sign up to learn various computer languages like C++ and Pascal using lessons you've developed. You've set up a page using Secure Socket Layer that accepts credit card information and creates user accounts using the Windows Scripting Host, but anonymous users are still able to get to your lessons because the logon prompt is never displayed to accept logon credentials. You've added the WebUsers group that contains all automatically created user accounts and verified that the IUSR_*computername* account is not present in the ACL of your Web site. Which of the following could secure your site?

   A. Check the "Require Basic Authentication" checkbox in the Web site's properties.

   B. Check the "Require Windows NT/Challenge Response" checkbox in the Web site's properties.

   C. Add the IUSR_*computername* account to the ACL of your Web site files.

   D. Remove the default Everyone/Full Control permission from the ACL of your Web site files.

   Answer: D. Everyone includes the IUSR_*computername* account, and it is established by default when NTFS volumes are formatted.

Resolve Index Server query problems.

Index Server works very well and is almost completely automatic. However, its behavior may not be what you expect. Sometimes the results of a query can seem strange.

Critical Information

Index Server problems fall into four categories, all but one of which are actually optimization problems:

- **Queries return files that shouldn't be returned.** This problem can be caused by NTFS file permissions that are not correctly set up or by filtering files of all types when you should be restricting filtering to known types.

- **Queries don't return files that they should.** This problem can be caused because the catalog may be restricted to certain virtual directories, because not all files are being filtered and some extensions are not registered for filtration, or because file permissions are limiting the files that the query returns. This is almost the exact opposite of the above condition.

- **Queries take too long to fulfill.** You might be able to correct this optimization problem by forcing master merges more often. Or you may simply have too many users. Consider creating more catalogs if your data doesn't need to be searched in a single index or moving data to another server. Using more powerful server hardware or removing other applications such as a database or mail server function will also help.

- **Queries time out or fail to return any data.** If the cause of this problem is an overloaded Index Server, outright failure will be foreshadowed by queries that take too long to fulfill. Other causes of this problem are network connectivity problems or corrupted Index Server files. If you've verified the connection between the host and the server, try reinstalling Index Server.

If your server runs out of RAM, Index Server will pause its current indexing and merging so as not to load the system. Queries will still operate, but new pages will not be indexed until the service restarts when more RAM is available.

If your computer runs low on available hard disk space while Index Server is running, it will gracefully degrade as follows:

- Index Server will not start an indexing operation unless it determines that there is probably enough memory to complete the operation.

- Shadow merges in progress will be aborted and retried when disk space is freed up.

- Master merges will be paused until more disk space is available. A master merge pause event will be written to the event log along with a disk full error.

TIP Index Server will pause indexing operations if it runs out of RAM. Index Server will pause merging operations if it runs out of disk space. Both will continue automatically when the system determines that more resources are available.

You can free up memory either by removing files from the corpus or by extending the volume set. In any case, you should not delete any files under the Index Server catalog directory in order to free up space. Index Server will detect additional space and resume indexing operations automatically.

Necessary Procedures

There are no necessary procedures for this objective.

Exam Essentials

Know when Index Server will pause during indexing. Index Server will pause while indexing if the computer runs out of memory. When more memory becomes available (due to lighter load or the shutdown of other services), indexing will continue.

Key Terms and Concepts

Catalog: The indexing data maintained by Index Server that contains the word list and the documents in which those words exist.

Corpus: The body of documents indexed by Index Server.

Indexing: The process of cataloging the location of words in a body of documents for cross-referencing.

Querying: The process of retrieving documents based on the presence of specific keywords in the body of the document.

Sample Questions

1. You install a new content filter in Index Server designed to display PostScript files. When you run a query using words that you know appear in Display PostScript Documents in your wwwroot directory, no Display PostScript files appear in the query. What should you do?

   A. Force a scan to activate the new content filter.

   B. Add the wwwroot directory to the Index Server list of scanned directories—it's not included by default.

   C. Force a Master Merge to include the catalog created for PostScript files.

   D. Create a new catalog for displaying PostScript files.

   Answer: A. Forcing a scan assures that newly installed content filters will index files of their respective type.

2. Your Index Server queries are returning CGI scripts as well as normal documents. How can you prevent this?

   A. Use NTFS file permissions to disallow access to CGI files for anonymous Internet users.

   B. Allow only Execute permissions to the CGI directories in the Directory Permissions window for all virtual directories.

C. Uncheck the CGI script virtual directories in the Index Server Manager.

D. Create multiple catalogs so that all CGI scripts appear in one catalog and all other content appears in another.

Answer: C. All other options either won't work or will restrict normal use of the CGI scripts.

Resolve setup issues when installing IIS on a Windows NT Server 4.0 computer.

Most installations of IIS4 will proceed successfully and uneventfully. Most problems that occur during installation can be solved by repairing the computer or making sure Windows NT itself is correctly installed. IIS4 is included in Windows NT Server 4 Option Pack, downloadable for free from Microsoft. IIS4 is a complete upgrade to IIS3 with the exception that the Gopher service is no longer supported and will be removed if you install IIS4.

Critical Information

If you have difficulty installing IIS4, the following checklist may help you figure out what is wrong:

- **Does the computer work?** IIS (and Windows NT) requires a stable hardware platform on which to run. Make sure that the computer is stable, without flaky memory or hard drive components, interrupt conflicts, or CPU bugs.

- **Is Windows NT installed correctly?** IIS needs a stable Windows NT platform on which to run. NT must also be informed of the actual configuration of hardware components. Ensure that NT is communicating with all of its components correctly.

- **Is the latest service pack installed?** IIS4 requires Service Pack 3. Install Service Pack 3 if it is not already present.

- **Does your computer have sufficient hard drive space?** IIS4 requires that your computer have at least 200MB of hard drive space, preferably much more. Check the free hard drive space on your server.

- **Is your computer powerful enough?** Microsoft recommends a Pentium 90 or faster microprocessor.

- **Does your computer have sufficient memory?** NT requires at least 32MB of memory and should have much more (see Chapter 2 for details) in order to run without performance degradation. Upgrade the memory in your server if it has less than 32MB.

After you troubleshoot the failed installation, determine the problem, and are ready to continue with the installation, the best thing to do is simply to restart the installation process. This will overwrite any previously installed files and produce a correct, complete installation of IIS4 on your server.

Necessary Procedures

There are no necessary procedures for this objective.

Exam Essentials

Know the minimum requirements and recommendations for running IIS. Microsoft recommends using a computer with no less than a 90MHz Intel Pentium processor, 32MB RAM, and 200MB remaining hard disk drive space, plus that required for your Web site files. Compute-intensive functions like Secure Socket Layer (SSL) encryption or busy sites will require more power.

Key Terms and Concepts

Option Pack: A major mid-life product upgrade that provides considerable added functionality to the operating system.

Service Pack: Periodically released collections of operating system fixes that correct bugs and add interim functionality between major releases of software. Equivalent to a patch in UNIX systems.

Sample Questions

1. You would like to upgrade your Internet service software from version 3.0 of Internet Information Server to version 4.0. You must, however, make sure that all of the Internet services you currently use on your Internet site will still be supported under version 4.0. Which of the following services is no longer supported under version 4.0 of IIS?

   A. HTTP

   B. FTP

   C. Gopher

   D. SNMP

   Answer: C

2. You have Windows NT version 4.0 (with Service Pack 3) and Internet Information Server version 3.0 installed on your Internet server computer. You want to upgrade to version 4.0 of IIS. What else do you need in order to install version 4.0 of IIS?

   A. Nothing. IIS is included for free on the Windows NT 4.0 Installation CD-ROM.

   B. Service Pack 4, which includes IIS4.

   C. Windows NT version 5.0 Beta 2.

   D. The Windows NT 4.0 Option Pack, which includes IIS4.

   Answer: D

3. You have just installed Windows NT Server 4.0 from the original installation CD-ROM on a 150MHz Intel Pentium computer with 96MB of RAM and 4GB of hard drive space. When you installed Windows NT you also installed Internet Information Server version 2.0. You have since applied Service Pack 2 to your Windows NT operating system. You attempt to install Internet Information Server 4.0 from the Windows NT Option Pack files you have downloaded from the Internet, but you are unsuccessful. Why?

   A. You must upgrade to version 3.0 of IIS before you install IIS4.

   B. You must install Service Pack 3 before you install IIS4.

   C. You do not have enough memory to install IIS4.

   D. Your processor is not powerful enough.

   Answer: B. IIS4 requires Service Pack 3.

4. You have just installed Windows NT Server 4.0 from the original installation CD-ROM on a 100MHz Intel 80486 computer with 32MB of RAM and 1.5GB of hard drive space. When you installed Windows NT you also installed Internet Information Server version 2.0. You have since applied Service Pack 3 to your Windows NT operating system. You are informed that Microsoft does not suggest that you install IIS4 on this system. Why?

   A. You must upgrade to version 3.0 of IIS before you install IIS4.

   B. You must install Service Pack 3 before you install IIS4.

   C. You do not have enough memory to install IIS4.

   D. Your processor is not powerful enough.

   Answer: D. Microsoft recommends at least a 90MHz Pentium.

5. You have just installed Windows NT Server 4.0 from the original installation CD-ROM on a 100MHz Intel Pentium computer with 24MB of RAM and 500MB of hard drive space. When you installed Windows NT you also installed Internet Information Server 2.0.

You have since applied Service Pack 3 to your Windows NT operating system. You are informed that Microsoft does not suggest that you install IIS4 on this system. Why?

A. You must upgrade to version 3.0 of IIS before you install IIS4.

B. You must install Service Pack 3 before you install IIS4.

C. You do not have enough memory to install IIS4.

D. Your processor is not powerful enough.

Answer: C. Microsoft recommends at least 32MB of RAM.

Use a WebMap to find and repair broken links.

The Site Server Express component of IIS provides a wealth of interesting information. For troubleshooting purposes, the real benefit of Site Server Express is its ability to search your Web map for problems such as broken links, "not found" objects, images without ALT tags, and large objects (which can cause a page to take a very long time to download).

Critical Information

As shown in Figure 7.1, Content Analyzer's Tools menu gives you the option to do a quick search on the following objects:

- Broken Links
- Home Site Objects
- Images Without ALT
- Load Size Over 32K
- Non-Home Site Objects

- Not Found Objects (404)
- Unavailable Objects
- Unverified Objects

FIGURE 7.1: You can search for missing Web items from the Tools menu

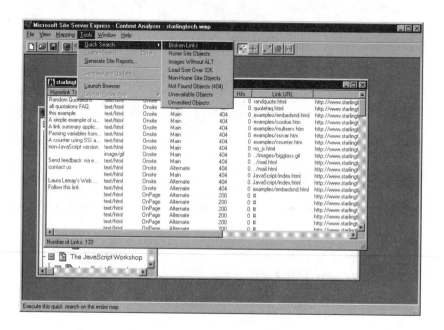

When you search on any one of these objects Site Server Express creates a search results window and lists those objects in it. When you click on the object in the search results window, the tree view and cyberbolic view automatically go to that object. You can then double-click on the object (or its parent if it is a broken link or a not-found object) to view the problem object or HTML page.

Site Server Express makes finding broken links easy. Then it is just a matter of fixing that link with the software you used to create the page, or perhaps just editing the file with a text editor, so that the link points to the correct location. Figure 7.2 shows the results of a link search.

FIGURE 7.2: Finding broken links with Content Analyzer

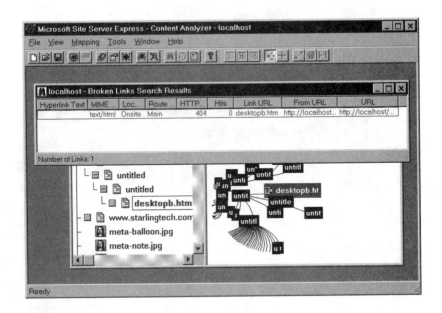

Necessary Procedures

Use the following procedure to find broken Web links in a Web site:

1. Launch the Content Analyzer.

2. Open or create a WebMap based on a Web site on your server.

3. Select Tools ➤ Quick Search ➤ Broken Links.

4. Record each file containing a broken link and the page to which the broken link refers.

5. Launch a text editor such as Notepad.

6. Open an HTML file containing a broken link.

7. Search for the name of the page to which the broken link refers, using the text editor's search menu option.

8. Change the found text to the name of an existing page.

9. Repeat steps 7 and 8 for each broken link in the file.

10. Repeat steps 6 through 9 for each file containing broken links.

11. Close the text editor.

12. Close all Content Analyzer documents.

13. Select File ➤ New ➤ Map From File.

14. Specify the same Web site as before.

15. Repeat this procedure from step 3 to verify that no broken links remain.

Exam Essentials

Know the purpose of Content Analyzer and why you would use it. Content Analyzer cross-checks the HTML documents that make up your Web site to ensure that it is self-consistent and that all links actually lead to available documents. Use Content Analyzer whenever you need to troubleshoot the operation of your site files rather than the operation of your server.

Know how to use Content Analyzer to search for broken links. Search for broken links using Content Analyzer's Tools ➤ Quick Search ➤ Broken Links option.

Key Terms and Concepts

Link: A URL embedded in a hypertext document; when the link is clicked on, the document it references will be automatically loaded and displayed.

Uniform Resource Locator (URL):   A syntax for uniquely identifying every document on the Internet.

Sample Questions

1. Users of your Web site complain that they often receive HTTP error 404. How can you eliminate this problem?

   A. Use Content Analyzer to search for orphan pages and delete them.

   B. Add the IUSR_*computername* account to the ACL for the pages that are being linked to.

   C. Use Report Writer to search for orphan pages and delete them.

   D. Use Content Analyzer to search for broken links and repair them.

   Answer: D. HTTP error 404 is the Not Found error.

Resolve WWW service problems.

After you've exhausted the preceding general troubleshooting tips, the following section on problems unique to the WWW service may provide additional help.

Critical Information

The following lists some commonly encountered problems and suggests ways to solve them. This list is by no means exhaustive but may give you a nudge in the right direction when you are perplexed.

- **Can't find your Web server.** No DNS entry. In order for Web browsers to find your Web site, your IIS computer must have a domain name entry in the DNS server responsible for your network. Use the command line NSLOOKUP.EXE tool to check for name records for any machine on the Internet.

- **Can't create a virtual Web site.** You must specify a unique port number, IP address, or host header for the Web site.

- **Can't require SSL.** You must have a certificate installed to require SSL for your Web site.

- **Can't select another IP address.** You must configure Windows NT Server to respond to additional IP addresses. This is done through the Network control panel.

- **Can't find server by other name.** In order for Web browsers to find your Web site, your IIS computer must have an entry corresponding to that name in the DNS server responsible for your network.

- **Browser can't find virtual site.** If you are using host headers, the browser must support host headers or you must use the CGI/ISAPI workaround. If you are using a port other than 80 on your Web site, any reference to that Web site must explicitly reference the port in the URL.

- **Browsers with plug-ins for multimedia data files or other types of data ask if you want to save the file to disk rather than displaying the data.** A MIME type must be defined for data types other than those already defined in the IIS default setup.

- **Site has moved and browsers can't find it.** You can redirect browsers to the new location of a Web site using the URL option in the Home Directory tab of the Web site's Properties sheet.

- **Users report that they get a logon prompt when they attempt to access the Web site but access is denied after they enter an account name and password.** You must have an account defined for the users if Anonymous Authentication is disabled.

- **You can't log on to the IIS Administrative Web site.** You must have Windows NT Challenge/Response enabled to use the administrative Web pages.

- **The anonymous user cannot access any files.** The anonymous account defined in the Web site Authentication Properties sheet must also exist and have the same password as a Windows NT account.

- **Browsers other than Internet Explorer are unable to be authenticated by your Web site.** Web browsers other than Internet Explorer require Basic Authentication to be authenticated as anything other than an anonymous user.

- **Users can't access Web site data stored on UNC share.** Be sure that share permissions are set correctly, and that an account name and password are established for Web site access to the share.

Necessary Procedures

Use the following procedure to add a MIME type:

1. Right-click on the server's icon in the scope pane of the MMC and select Properties.

2. Click the File Types button.

3. Click New Type.

4. Enter **non** in the Associated Extension input box.

5. Enter **non-existent type** in the Content Type (MIME) input box.

6. Click OK.

7. Click OK.

8. Click OK.

Use the following procedure to install a digital certificate on your Web site using Certificate Server:

1. Right-click on the Web site you want to install a certificate on and select Properties.

2. Click the Directory Security tab.

3. Click the Key Manager button.

4. Right-click the WWW service and select Create New Key....

5. Accept Automatically Send the Request to an On-Line Authority and click the Next button.

6. Enter **test key** in the Key Name field.

7. Enter **test** in the Password field.

8. Enter **test** again in the Confirm Password field.

9. Click the Next button.

10. Enter **test company** in the Organization field.

11. Enter **test division** in the Organizational Unit field.

12. Enter the fully qualified domain name that will be used by Web browsers to access the Web site in the Common Name field.

13. Click the Next button.

14. Enter your country in the Country field.

15. Enter your state or province in the State/Province field.

16. Enter your city or locality in the City/Locality field.

17. Click the Finish button. The certificate will be automatically submitted to the Certificate Server on your IIS computer if you installed Certificate Server. Click OK.

18. Click the Add... button.

19. Accept the Any Unassigned IP Address and Any Unassigned Port options and click the OK button.

20. Click OK again.

21. Select Commit Changes Now from the Computers menu.

22. Select Exit from the Computers menu.

23. In the Properties tab for the Web site, click the Secure Communications Edit... button again.

24. Check the Require Secure Channel When Using This Resource button.

25. Click OK.

26. Click Apply.

27. Click OK.

Exam Essentials

Know how and when to add MIME types to a server. Add MIME types whenever users complain that browsers are querying for a save-to-disk filename rather than being displayed. Add MIME types through the IIS server Master Properties window.

Know how to set up secure posting. Configure a Web site to require SSL through the Secure Communications area of the Directory Security Properties window.

Key Terms and Concepts

Multipurpose Internet Mail Extension (MIME) type: A method for specifying the content of a file based on its filename extension. When an HTTP server transmits a file, it precedes the file with a MIME type that specifies what type of content is being transmitted. The MIME type used is based on the filename extension of the content—for example, `.bmp` files are of MIME type bitmap.

Plug-in: An extension to a Web browser that handles the display of a specific MIME type. For instance, the Acrobat plug-in from Adobe displays the MIME type PostScript Display Format (`.pdf`) files.

Sample Questions

1. You want anonymous access to your new virtual Web site to be done through a different anonymous access account than the default Web site uses, so you enter a new anonymous account name and password in the Directory Security portion of the Web site's Properties window. After you do this users are no longer able to access the Web site anonymously. What is wrong?

   A. You must reboot your Web server computer for the changes to take effect.

B. The default anonymous account name and password for all Web services is overriding the password you have selected for that specific Web site. Remove the account name and password from the anonymous account settings at the computer level.

C. The account must be one of those listed in the Operators tab for the Web site.

D. You must also create the anonymous account using the User Manager or User Manager for Domains program and assign it the same password that you used in IIS. The account must also have Log on locally rights.

Answer: D. The account must also exist as a Windows NT account, and IIS will not create it for you. Do *not* make the anonymous account also an operator for the Web site—that would allow anyone to change your Web site settings!

2. You have established an archive of .mp3 compressed audio files, making them available for download to browsers of your Web site. People browsing your site, even those with MP3 plug-ins for their Web browsers, report that their Web browsers will not play the file. The browsers instead ask if the users want to save the file. How can you best fix this problem?

A. Install an MP3 compression ISAPI DLL in the ISAPI Filters tab of the Web site.

B. Rename all the .mp3 files to have the extension .mpg.

C. Add the file extension .mp3 and the MIME type audio/x-mpeg to the MIME types in the HTTP Headers tab of the Web site.

D. Use an audio utility program to convert all the MP3 files to .au files.

Answer: C. The Web browser must be informed about what kind of file is being sent to it. IIS determines what to tell the browser by the file's extension and the associated MIME type in the MIME map.

Resolve FTP service problems.

Most FTP service problems fall under the general trouble-shooting steps already covered for the other services. The process for troubleshooting FTP service problems is pretty much the same as for any other service.

Critical Information

When you have FTP service problems and you've gone through normal troubleshooting procedures, test your installation against the following questions:

- Is the IIS installation complete, uncorrupted, and running?

- For directory- or access-related problems, are directory permissions set the way they should be on both the home directory and the directory in question?

- For access problems, are the IUSR_*computername* account permissions and rights (especially the Log on locally user right) set correctly?

- Have you stopped and started the FTP service after adding a virtual directory?

- For custom client connection problems, have you set the directory listing style to UNIX?

- If certain clients can't attach to your FTP site running on an unusual port, is the client capable of attaching to an FTP server that is not running on port 21? You must specify the FTP port number when attaching with a client if your FTP service is not running on port 21.

NOTE   The IUSR_*computername* account must have Log on locally rights for Internet users to be able to log in.

You may also need to limit the bandwidth the IIS service uses if you use the same server for other functions, such as file service. You may find that IIS traffic is consuming an inordinate amount of network bandwidth if (for example) you share a T1 connection to the Internet for remote connectivity to another site.

Necessary Procedures

Use the following procedure to specify UNIX as the directory listing style:

1. Select Start ➤ Windows NT 4 Option Pack ➤ Microsoft Internet Information Server ➤ Internet Service Manager.

2. Expand the Internet Information Server node to show the active sites on your server.

3. Right-click on the test FTP site you created earlier and select Properties.

4. Select the Home Directory tab.

5. Select UNIX in the Directory Listing Style.

6. Click OK.

7. Right-click on the test FTP site and select Stop.

8. Right-click on the test FTP site and select Start.

9. Close the MMC.

Use the following procedure to limit service bandwidth for all IIS traffic:

1. Select Start ➤ Windows NT 4 Option Pack ➤ Microsoft Internet Information Server ➤ Internet Service Manager.

2. Expand the Internet Information Server node to show your server.

3. Right-click on your server.

4. Select Properties.

5. Check Enable Bandwidth Throttling.

6. Enter **10** in the Maximum network use input box.

7. Click OK.

8. Close the MMC.

Exam Essentials

Know how to resolve FTP client compatibility issues. Many FTP clients are only capable of connecting to FTP servers that run on port 21.

Know how and when to specify the UNIX style directory listing. Most graphical FTP clients rely on having strict UNIX style directory listings returned from the server. These clients will not function correctly when the MS-DOS directory listing style is specified in the FTP site's properties.

Key Terms and Concepts

Directory Listing Style: The specific manner in which FTP directory contents are returned to the client. Two styles exist that mimic the command line displays of native directory commands: UNIX and MS-DOS. Of the two, UNIX is the far more widely used and compatible.

Sample Questions

1. Anonymous FTP users complain that they can't log in. You've recently changed the password for the IUSR_computername account because you suspect it may have been compromised. How can you solve this problem?

   A. Require Challenge/Response Authentication.

   B. Require Basic Authentication.

   C. Enable SSL Encryption.

   D. Enable password synchronization for the FTP service.

   Answer: D. You should enable password synchronization so the password your service uses to log in is always correct.

2. Some Internet users complain that they can't see directory listings from your Web site. When you have them connect to the FTP site using the Microsoft FTP client built into Windows NT, they have no problems. What can you do to solve this problem?

   A. Tell your users that IIS FTP service is only compatible with the Microsoft client.

   B. Tell your users to use a Web browser to connect to the service and specify the FTP protocol in the URL.

   C. Tell your users to upgrade to a better FTP client.

   D. Specify the UNIX directory listing style in the MMC FTP snap-in.

   Answer: D. Never rely on your users to change their software to suit your site unless they are employees of your own company.

3. You've changed your FTP service port to 2121 so as not to conflict with an FTP proxy running on your IIS machine. Your users complain that they can't reach your FTP site now. What should you do?

   A. Instruct users to put the port number 2121 after the IP address or domain name when they connect to your FTP site.

   B. Stop and start the FTP services.

C. Reinstall the FTP service.

D. This is a trick question. FTP only runs on port 21.

Answer: A. Users will have to specify the port number of your FTP site if you move it off the standard port 21.

Index

NOTE: Page numbers in *italic* refer to figures or tables; page numbers in **bold** refer to significant discussions of the topic

MCSE EXAM NOTES®

MCSE Exam Notes:
NT SERVER 4

EXAM 70-067

FULL COVERAGE OF EACH
EXAM OBJECTIVE

KNOW WHAT YOU NEED TO
KNOW—AND NAIL THE EXAM

INCLUDES EXAM-TAKING
STRATEGIES

Microsoft Certified
Professional
Approved Study Guide

ISBN: 0-7821-2289-2
384 pp; 5⁷/8" x 8¹/4"; Softcover
$19.99

MCSE Exam Notes:
NT SERVER 4
IN THE ENTERPRISE

EXAM 70-068

FULL COVERAGE OF EACH
EXAM OBJECTIVE

KNOW WHAT YOU NEED TO
KNOW—AND NAIL THE EXAM

INCLUDES EXAM-TAKING
STRATEGIES

Microsoft Certified
Professional
Approved Study Guide

ISBN: 0-7821-2292-2
416 pp; 5⁷/8" x 8¹/4"; Softcover
$19.99

THE FASTEST AND MOST EFFECTIVE WAY TO MAKE SURE YOU'RE READY FOR THE MCSE EXAMS:

- Unique, innovative approach helps you gain and retain the knowledge you need, objective by objective.

- Essential information is arranged for quick learning and review.

- Exam tips and advice are offered by expert trainers.

OTHER TITLES INCLUDE:
MCSE Exam Notes™: NT® Workstation 4
MCSE Exam Notes™: Networking Essentials
MCSE Exam Notes™: Windows® 95
MCSE Exam Notes™: TCP/IP for NT® Server 4
MCSE Exam Notes™: Exchange Server 5.5
MCSE Exam Notes™: Internet Information Server 4
MCSE Exam Notes™: SQL Server 6.5 Administration
MCSE Exam Notes™: Proxy Server 2
MCSE Exam Notes™: Systems Management Server

CORE BOX SET ALSO AVAILABLE:
MCSE Exam Notes™: Core Requirements box set
- 4 books:
    MCSE Exam Notes™: Networking Essentials
    MCSE Exam Notes™: NT® Workstation 4
    MCSE Exam Notes™: NT® Server 4
    MCSE Exam Notes™: NT® Server 4 in the Enterprise
- Bonus CD
- Only $64.99—Save $15.00

NETWORK PRESS®
SYBEX

www.sybex.com

MCSE CORE REQUIREMENT STUDY GUIDE FROM NETWORK PRESS®

Sybex's Network Press presents updated and expanded second editions of the definitive study guides for MCSE candidates.

ISBN: 0-7821-2220-5
704pp; 7¹/₂" x 9"; Hardcover
$49.99

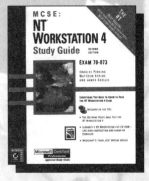

ISBN: 0-7821-2223-X
784pp; 7¹/₂" x 9"; Hardcover
$49.99

ISBN: 0-7821-2222-1
832pp; 7¹/₂" x 9"; Hardcover
$49.99

ISBN: 0-7821-2221-3
704pp; 7¹/₂" x 9"; Hardcover
$49.99

ISBN: 0-7821-2256-6
800pp; 7¹/₂" x 9"; Hardcover
$49.99

A $50.00 SAVINGS!

MCSE Core Requirements
Box Set
ISBN: 0-7821-2245-0
4 hardcover books;
3,024pp total; $149.96

Microsoft® Certified
Professional
Approved Study Guide

NETWORK PRESS®
SYBEX

STUDY GUIDES FOR THE MICROSOFT CERTIFIED SYSTEMS ENGINEER EXAM

MCSE ELECTIVE STUDY GUIDES FROM NETWORK PRESS®

Sybex's Network Press expands the definitive study guide series for MCSE candidates.

MCSE: TCP/IP FOR NT SERVER 4 STUDY GUIDE
THIRD EDITION
EXAM 70-059

ISBN: 0-7821-2224-8
688pp; 7¹/₂" x 9"; Hardcover
$49.99

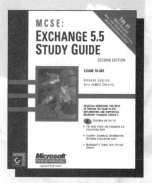

MCSE: EXCHANGE 5.5 STUDY GUIDE
SECOND EDITION
EXAM 70-081

ISBN: 0-7821-2261-2
848pp; 7¹/₂" x 9"; Hardcover
$49.99

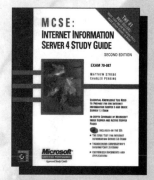

MCSE: INTERNET INFORMATION SERVER 4 STUDY GUIDE
SECOND EDITION
EXAM 70-087

ISBN: 0-7821-2248-5
704pp; 7¹/₂" x 9"; Hardcover
$49.99

MCSE: SQL SERVER 6.5 ADMINISTRATION STUDY GUIDE

ISBN: 0-7821-2172-1
672pp; 7¹/₂" x 9"; Hardcover
$49.99

MCSE: PROXY SERVER 2 Study Guide
EXAM 70-088

ISBN: 0-7821-2194-2
576pp; 7¹/₂" x 9"; Hardcover
$49.99

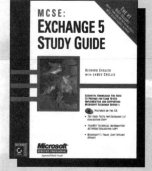

MCSE: EXCHANGE 5 STUDY GUIDE

ISBN: 0-7821-1967-0
656pp; 7¹/₂" x 9"; Hardcover
$49.99

Microsoft Certified Professional
Approved Study Guide

NETWORK PRESS® SYBEX

'UDY GUIDES FOR THE MICROSOFT CERTIFIED SYSTEMS ENGINEER EXAMS

NETWORK PRESS® PRESENTS
MCSE TEST SUCCESS®

THE PERFECT COMPANION BOOKS TO THE MCSE STUDY GUIDES

MCSE Test Success:
NETWORKING ESSENTIALS
EXAM 70-058
TODD LAMMLE

GET READY FOR THE EXAM—OBJECTIVE BY OBJECTIVE
MASTER ALL THE MATERIAL YOU NEED TO KNOW
PRACTICE ON 500 REVIEW QUESTIONS AND SAMPLE TEST QUESTIONS

ISBN: 0-7821-2146-2
352pp; 7¹/₂" x 9"; Softcover
$24.99

MCSE Test Success:
NT SERVER 4
EXAM 70-067
LISA DONALD

GET READY FOR THE EXAM—OBJECTIVE BY OBJECTIVE
MASTER ALL THE MATERIAL YOU NEED TO KNOW
PRACTICE ON 500 REVIEW QUESTIONS AND SAMPLE TEST QUESTIONS

ISBN: 0-7821-2148-9
352pp; 7¹/₂" x 9"; Softcover
$24.99

MCSE Test Success:
NT WORKSTATION 4
EXAM 70-073
TODD LAMMLE
LISA DONALD

GET READY FOR THE EXAM—OBJECTIVE BY OBJECTIVE
MASTER ALL THE MATERIAL YOU NEED TO KNOW
PRACTICE ON 950 REVIEW QUESTIONS AND SAMPLE TEST QUESTIONS

ISBN: 0-7821-2149-7
400pp; 7¹/₂" x 9"; Softcover
$24.99

MCSE Test Success:
NT SERVER 4 IN THE ENTERPRISE
EXAM 70-068
LISA DONALD

GET READY FOR THE EXAM—OBJECTIVE BY OBJECTIVE
MASTER ALL THE MATERIAL YOU NEED TO KNOW
PRACTICE ON MORE THAN 500 REVIEW QUESTIONS AND SAMPLE TEST QUESTIONS

ISBN: 0-7821-2147-0
442pp; 7¹/₂" x 9"; Softcover
$24.99

Here's what you n to know to pass th MCSE tests.

- Review concise summ of key information

- Boost your knowledge with 400 review quest

- Get ready for the test 200 tough practice tes questions

Other MCSE Test Success titles:

- **Core Requirements** (4 books, 1 CD)
  [ISBN: 0-7821-2296-5]

- **Windows® 95**
  [ISBN: 0-7821-2252-3]

- **Exchange Server 5.5**
  [ISBN: 0-7821-2250-7]

- **TCP/IP for NT® 4**
  [ISBN: 0-7821-2251-5]

Microsoft Certified
Professional
Approved Study Guide

NETWORK PRESS® SYBEX